"I know of no one who cares less for the superficial 'worries of this life' (Mt 13:22) than Marlena Graves. She is a voice calling out in our generation, beckoning us to a vision of Christ that has nearly been drowned out by the rise of self-help pseudo-Christianity. And this book? This book is her heart on paper. If you want to sit under a spiritual giant, and if you want to remember just what kind of freedom we are called to in Christ, do not miss this message."

Sharon Hodde Miller, author of *Nice: Why We Love to Be Liked and How God Calls Us to More*

"We have forgotten the way of Jesus—this one who 'calls us to stoop,' writes Marlena Graves. In her newest book, *The Way Up Is Down*, Graves's voice is bold and prophetic, calling each of us out of the wilderness of self-will to repent of our lust for power and material greed. But this isn't just a book. It's the compelling witness of a life: a woman born into poverty and racial oppression, who sees and loves the lowly and invites us to become like them."

Jen Pollock Michel, author of *Surprised by Paradox* and *Keeping Place*

"It is a rare and sacred gift for a writer to serve her raw heart—tender and salted with tears—to nourish the world. *The Way Up Is Down* is a profound act of Christlike service. Honest, poignant, and lyrical, this is a book that shows what it tells. It's unforgettable, incisive, and deeply needed. Thank you, Marlena, for sharing your precious gift—your story, your yearning for a better way. I am inspired."

Paul J. Pastor, author of *The Face of the Deep*, *The Listening Day*, and *Palau: A Life on Fire*

"This honest and intimate book reveals the truth of God's humility and invites us all into God's wonders. What an important read for the modern Christian!"

Julia Walsh, Franciscan Sister of Perpetual Adoration, author and retreat leader

"In a world clamoring for spotlight, status, and success, Marlena helpfully calls us back to the ancient wisdom of the church: that true life is found in dying and true significance in giving yourself away. Jesus is our trailblazer as we embark on this path of the kingdom, whose own way up to exaltation was found through laying down his life for us, and he beckons us to now follow in his stead."

Joshua Ryan Butler, pastor of Redemption Church, Tempe, author of *The Skeletons in God's Closet*

"In *The Way Up Is Down*, Marlena reminds us that we serve the world well when we are emptied out. Through powerful stories and thoughtful prompts, she asks us to consider what it means to follow a Jesus who often does what we least expect—who serves and loves in a way that turns everything upside down. I'm grateful for her voice in this world."

Kaitlin Curtice, Potawatomi author and speaker

"A book that will challenge every perception of leadership. Marlena takes you through a journey of emptying your privilege, power obsession, position climbing, and the multifaceted pecking order to discover a holy exchange. It will literally wreck your soul. *The Way Up Is Down* is a sacred interlude that will lead readers into a holy place of vulnerability. It will cause you to reframe and define what it means to be an authentic leader in a world distracted with vain celebrity culture."

Gricel Medina, leadership and community developer, Midsouth Conference of the Evangelical Covenant Church

The Way Up Is Down

BECOMING YOURSELF BY FORGETTING YOURSELF

MARLENA GRAVES

An imprint of InterVarsity Press
Downers Grove, Illinois

InterVarsity Press
P.O. Box 1400, Downers Grove, IL 60515-1426
ivpress.com
email@ivpress.com

InterVarsity Press® is the book-publishing division of InterVarsity Christian Fellowship/USA®, a movement of students and faculty active on campus at hundreds of universities, colleges, and schools of nursing in the United States of America, and a member movement of the International Fellowship of Evangelical Students. For information about local and regional activities, visit intervarsity.org.

All Scripture quotations, unless otherwise indicated, are taken from The Holy Bible, New International Version®, NIV®. Copyright © 1973, 1978, 1984, 2011 by Biblica, Inc.™ Used by permission of Zondervan. All rights reserved worldwide. www.zondervan. com. The "NIV" and "New International Version" are trademarks registered in the United States Patent and Trademark Office by Biblica, Inc.™

While any stories in this book are true, some names and identifying information may have been changed to protect the privacy of individuals.

Cover design and image composite: Cindy Kiple
Interior design: Jeanna Wiggins
Images: blue ocean painting: @Saemilee/Digital Vision Vectors/Getty Images

ISBN 978-0-8308-4674-0 (print)
ISBN 978-0-8308-4675-7 (digital)

Printed in the United States of America ♾

Library of Congress Cataloging-in-Publication Data

A catalog record for this book is available from the Library of Congress.

P 23 22 21 20 19 18 17 16 15 14 13 12 11 10 9 8 7 6 5 4 3 2 1
Y 38 37 36 35 34 33 32 31 30 29 28 27 26 25 24 23 22 21 20

For mi familia:

those preceding me, my parents, siblings,

Shawn, Iliana, Valentina, and Isabella—

God's delight.

Contents

1

Self-Emptying

THE MYSTERY OF OUR SALVATION

*The entire mystery of the economy
of our salvation consists in the self-emptying
and abasement of the Son of God.*

ST. CYRIL OF ALEXANDRIA

*If I could become the servant of all,
no lower place to fall.*

MEWITHOUTYOU, "JANUARY 1979"

I stood alone at our kitchen counter staring out the window at the menacing gray clouds. I read God the riot act: "Lord, nothing is left! I am empty. Barren. Your people or the scoundrels who claim to be—and you know I have more choice words for them than that in my heart—are a cabal of arsonists who set fire to our entire Christian community. We did nothing wrong and yet you let them burn it down to the ground. And then let them off scot-free! We've given up everything to follow you. For once could the meek inherit the earth instead of being trampled on?"

It seems like God always has me carrying one cross or another. I'm putting one down just to pick another up.

I continued my litany of complaints: "What glory is there in this? What more do you want from me? I have nothing left to give. N-O-T-H-I-N-G. On empty. Bone dry. Just change my name to 'Mara' because with Naomi I am bitter."

A moment later I threw down the gauntlet: "Is this how you treat your friends?"

The question is one I stole from St. Teresa of Ávila. The story goes that Theresa was traveling with a band of priests and nuns. She was on her way to start a new convent. As the holy party crossed a stream, her donkey launched her into the air and she fell off. At that moment she heard the Lord say to her, "That is how I treat my friends." Without skipping a beat, she retorted, "That is why you have so few of them." Oh, how I can identify with her response! Another time she described life as a "night spent at an uncomfortable inn." When I tried that line on God, telling him that my life too felt like an uncomfortable inn, the Lord quickly countered with, "Well, at least you have somewhere to lay your head. And at least there's room at the inn for you." I was like, "I see how you are."

I take my permission to speak freely to God from the Bible, especially the psalmists and the great cloud of witnesses throughout history. I spend my days and nights telling him what I think—prayers, praises, laments, disgusts with evangelical and national politics, depressions, dreams, and inside jokes.

Sometimes we find ourselves in side-splitting laughter, especially when well-intentioned souls sing fervently but horribly off-key in church. When that happens, I lose my composure every single time. I laugh so hard that I shake, with tears running down my face. Then I have to exit my pew to flee to the restroom and regain my composure. My worst nightmare is when I am helping to lead the service and someone is singing loudly off-key. Beside myself, I look down as if I am praying or quietly contemplating what is being sung. Only I am not. I am trying not to die laughing and hoping not to make anyone feel bad or to distract the congregation, which, thankfully, has only happened once. But that's a story for another time.

On other occasions I'm overcome by God's holiness and lie flat on my face—prostrate, no words—speechless, for God is holy other. *Mysterium tremendum.*

ALWAYS ON MY MIND

When I was little, my dad, whom I love deeply, would get in the silliest of moods. He attempted to humor me and my siblings, and also express love, with his rendition of iconic country singer Willie Nelson's song "Always on My Mind." Mostly my dad humored himself. My sister Michelle and brothers Kenny and Marco and I clapped our ears. He sounded more like a howling wolf. Maybe that's why I can't control myself when someone sings way off tune.

But I suppose that if I were to fiddle with the lyrics of the song by changing *were* to *are*, I could serenade God with "You are always on my mind. You are always on my mind." Father, Son, and Holy Spirit—God in three persons, blessed Trinity— are always and ever on my mind. The triune God is always on my mind wherever I am and in whatever condition I find myself even if I read him the riot act and he chooses to plead the Fifth.

When God is silent and darkness covers the face of my earth, I just take a number and stand in a long line with the rest of them—Job, Jesus, and all those throughout millennia who've had God plead the Fifth on them. My greatest of tantrums, most brilliant protests, and intestine-twisting agonies seldom pry a straight answer or any answer at all out of him when I want one.

Even though I think I know that, after so long I find I am unable to wait anymore in the waiting room of life. So, I shoot up from the chair and try a different tactic. I pace back and forth like a caged animal. Stomp on the floor. Make all the noise I can. Wave my hands like a fool trying different antics to get God's attention. When that doesn't work, I head straight to God's door and start asking, seeking, and knocking. No, *pounding*. "I know you're in there. When you gonna show your face?" I figure I'll be the persistent widow. But God persists in responding in his own time, in his own way, and on his own terms. I am forced to sit down again, to trust him instead of giving in to despair while he has the right to remain silent. I can't stand it. Most of the time I can only trust him in the new round of waiting with the help of others. On my own, I fall apart. And yet even the waiting room of my life remains God-haunted. Really, what I am is God-intoxicated, a staggering drunk.

My daily and desperate need for him and the physical hunger I sometimes experienced as a child—emptiness—was sort of an involuntary fast. It all coalesced into my constant awareness of the manifest presence of God, into his always being on my mind, ever before me. And yet, on some days, I still find myself empty. I do things like read God the riot act and insinuate his betrayal. How can this be?

I don't know.

Just like I don't know how Satan could have turned from God. Or how Adam and Eve could've sinned when they had everything they could have ever wanted in God. Or how Judas could've betrayed Jesus after spending three years with him. Or how Peter betrayed Jesus to his face shortly after promising he never would.

What if I, like Adam, Eve, Judas, and Peter, have everything I could possibly ever want right now in God and just don't see what is right in front of me? What if I am refusing to see it?

JESUS' WAY: EMPTY THAT WE MAY BE FULL

After I read God the riot act in my kitchen, I had no more to say. I quit talking. Eventually, in the silence between us, I heard him respond to me in a faint whisper. This is one time when he didn't plead the Fifth. This is what he said: "Only when you are empty, can you be made full." And "My strength is made perfect in your weakness."

That is not what I wanted to hear.

Only recently have I begun to awaken to the depths of this word to me, its particularities, and to the knowledge that being emptied in order for God to fill me (and any one of us) is the pathway to deeper communion with him. It leads us to the depths and glories of the kingdom.

Wake up, sleeper,
     rise from the dead,
          and Christ will shine on you. (Ephesians 5:14)

God's riptide is intent on moving me further and further away from the shores of self-centeredness. In the ocean of grace I cannot cling to my will or the illusions I possess; I have to swim by living into the fullness of reality. God is intent on making me more real, a less-distorted image of him. As I become more like him, I become more human. In turn, I will love him and others with a deeper love. I will become dependent on God to energize me with his life.

If I want to be full, open to receiving abundant grace—more human, selfless—first I must be emptied. He must increase, and I must decrease (John 3:30 ESV). The word I discovered is *kenōsis*. Oh, it's not that I never heard the word. On the contrary, I'm quite familiar with the idea. But it's one thing to define it and discuss it in a detached sort of way—to keep it at a safe distance. It's another thing altogether when God calls us to put it into practice. And he always calls us to put it into practice.

Kenōsis is a voluntary self-emptying, a renunciation of my will in favor of God's. It's a life characterized by self-giving. It is the kind of yielding Mary, Mother of God, displayed in her tender and trust-filled acceptance of God's birth announcement delivered by the angel Gabriel. "'I am the Lord's servant,' Mary answered. 'May your word to me be fulfilled'" (Luke 1:38). Mary embraced poverty of self-will with a spirit of humility even when she had no idea what was happening and no guarantee that all would turn out well. Nevertheless, she risked everything on God. She gave herself over to God's plans for her life instead of plotting her own. I wonder, *Could I be like Mary?*

> **God is intent on making me more real, a less-distorted image of him.**

6

And could it be that Jesus learned the habit of voluntary self-emptying and renunciation of self-will by observing his mother? In relinquishing his own will for the sake of the Father's will throughout his earthly life, Jesus exhibited the same posture of his mother: "I am the Lord's servant. . . . May your word to me be fulfilled."

Jesus' trust in our Father's good will was tested over and over again. Our trust will be too. And yet God calls us to the same kind of life posture Jesus had:

> Have this mind among yourselves, which is yours in Christ Jesus, who, though he was in the form of God, did not count equality with God a thing to be grasped, but emptied himself, taking the form of a servant, being born in the likeness of men. And being found in human form he humbled [emptied] himself and became obedient to the point of death, even death on a cross. (Philippians 2:5-8 ESV)

Jesus didn't cling to his rights. He repeatedly gave them up. His posture was "Not my will, but yours be done" (Luke 22:42). Similarly, each day of our lives God asks us to relinquish our rights in favor of his will—that our will and his will may become one. To choose emptiness entails a deep trust in God as we take the downward descent into servanthood and humility. We give up the endeavor of propping up ourselves. This ladder of success is inverted. This is the path of Jesus and of his disciples. It is the way of his mama. But it makes absolutely no sense from the human perspective.

Servanthood marked by this self-emptying, selflessness, or *kenōsis* begins with the surrender of our wills to God. Little by little in the strength of the Holy Spirit, we submissively

renounce our self-will and cooperate with God to empty ourselves of our Godless selves that we might be filled with God's

> **To choose emptiness entails a deep trust in God as we take the downward descent into servanthood and humility.**

life. It is the Galatians 2:20-21 life.
I learned this one in the KJV: "I
am crucified with Christ: nevertheless I live; yet not I, but Christ
liveth in me: and the life which I
now live in the flesh I live by the
faith of the Son of God, who
loved me, and gave himself for me." Notice Paul points out that
Jesus gave, or offered himself up, for Paul (and you and me)
out of love. That's what we're talking about here. It is a life
characterized by offering ourselves out of love for God, others,
and creation. We surrender to God so he might live in and
through us. Our lives become a love offering. Plain and simple.

But not so simple.

Sometimes we don't want to do what God calls us to do.
We fear the heavy toll it will take on us. Life already has us
ragged. If we're honest with ourselves, we know we are habituated toward being self-serving instead of self-giving. We
are inclined to choose ourselves first over God. We'd prefer
to give God and others orders instead of taking them. Moreover, we worry that self-offering won't get us anywhere in the
world or in the church. It probably won't. There won't be any
standing ovations or saintly Nobel Peace Prizes awarded or
even measly high-fives. Offering ourselves as living sacrifices
(Romans 12:1-2), our heroic deaths, the kinds that legends are
made of, will pass by mostly unnoticed by others. Yet our love
and obedience are never wasted. One day they will be richly
rewarded (I Corinthians 15:58).

Caryll Houselander writes,

> Many people feel that they could achieve heroic sanctity
> if they could do it in the way that appeals to them, for
> example, by being martyred. They can picture themselves
> cheerfully going to the stake . . . but if God makes no
> revelation but just lets them go on carrying out an insig-
> nificant job in the office day after day, or asks them to go
> on being gentle to a crotchety husband, or to continue
> to be a conscientious housemaid, they are not willing.
> They do not trust God to know his own will for them.

Hearing the call to renounce our wills in each new circumstance so God's will can be done in and through every part of
us is the call to selflessness. It's not a one-time deal. It requires
daily repentance and conversion to the ways of God. We'll
constantly have to examine ourselves and decide whether we
really want to go Jesus' way and surrender all control of the
outcomes to God. Maybe like Peter we make grand promises
at the beginning, tell Jesus that we'll go to any lengths for him,
follow him anywhere, that we'd die for him. And then when
push comes to shove and life doesn't turn out the way we want
it to—when we finally realize what is at stake—we backpedal.
We swear up and down that we don't know Jesus or what he
is about or that it would require so much of us. Maybe we read
God the riot act. We continue in this vein until some rooster in
the distance shocks us awake to the reality of things, and then
we are beside ourselves with sorrow and self-recrimination.

Or maybe our initial reaction is to run away (or want to run
away) from it. We're Jonahs hopping aboard the first ship to
Tarshish. We're like my three-year-old daughter, Isabella, who

has gotten into the habit of fleeing from me, of running away and hiding if she doesn't want to do what I have asked. She is bound and determined that her will be done, not mine.

There's always surrender to humiliation and crucifixion, an emptying, before the glory. There's no way around it. For my own part, I wish there were. Emptiness comes before fullness. We have to empty ourselves of anything that crowds out the life or grace of God in our lives. When we cooperate with the Spirit in this way, we become receptacles of grace. Like Jesus' mother Mary, we become God-bearers, pregnant with the divine. We are rich toward God and others. Filled full.

All this makes sense of why God told Paul, "My grace is sufficient for you, for my power is made perfect in weakness." And it explains why Paul could truthfully write, "Therefore I will boast all the more gladly about my weaknesses, so that Christ's power may rest on me. That is why, for Christ's sake, I delight in weaknesses, in insults, in hardships, in persecutions, in difficulties. For when I am weak, then I am strong" (2 Corinthians 12:9-11). Paul knew that God's strength could be unleashed in his weakness, that when he was empty, he was in the perfect position to be filled with God's power. In acknowledging and admitting our emptiness, being poor in spirit and contrite in heart, in taking the posture of a servant, we too can become open to realizing God's strength and power in us and in the kingdom. When we are full of ourselves or other things, we obstruct God's grace.

Father Stephen Freeman, an Eastern Orthodox priest, writes, "If we are to be transformed 'from one degree of glory to another' then it is towards the 'glory' of the crucified, self-emptying Christ that we are being transformed. . . . For there is no other kind of life revealed to us in Christ." Crucifixion and self-emptying—there is no other kind of Christian life. This is the life God calls us to. And it takes practice. It takes God's strength.

In the following pages, we'll explore ways in which God is calling you and me to surrender continually to being emptied and then filled with his abounding grace. We'll soon discover that this is the process whereby saints are made. This is the selfless-way, the God-shaped life.

2

Down Low with Jesus

Jesus has so diligently searched for the lowest place that
it would be very difficult for anyone to tear it from him.

FATHER CHARLES DE FOUCAULD

None of us knows what we don't know unless our eyes are
opened. My first revelation was the cafeteria lunch ticket.
It was on display for all to see when I handed it to the lunch
lady. No way to be discrete. Its bright color marked me as eli-
gible for a free lunch.

Sometimes sheer embarrassment over being known as poor
kept me from eating lunch. My free lunch ticket: a stigma. Of
course, if I were really hungry and knew I'd return home to an
empty refrigerator when I stepped off of the school bus, I swallowed my pride and presented the lunch ticket.

More indications.

Upon returning from Puerto Rico in fifth grade, someone
derogatorily asked, "Are you black?" Until then, I didn't know
I looked different from others. Now, as a bleached out biracial

Puerto Rican, I am *blanquita*. Then, I was darker. As a child and teenager, I didn't know I had an accent until my best friend's mother told me I did. Now, I am told I have no accent.

However, it was as an employee at a Christian college that I became acutely aware of the economic, cultural, and racial disparity in my environments. It was at the Christian college that I learned how underprivileged I was.

After Brenda Salter-McNeil, a thought leader in the area of racial reconciliation, led a large room full of people in an activity dubbed the "Race Race," everything made sense. The starting line was masking tape laid down across the middle of an all-purpose classroom. Dr. Salter-McNeil asked a series of questions like: Did you go to summer camps? Did your parents attend college? Did you qualify for free and reduced lunches? Are you a woman? and Are you an ethnic minority? Our answers determined whether we took steps forward or backward.

At the end of fifty questions, I was at the back of the room with one of my best friends, an African American woman. Almost dead last. Way behind the starting line, not to mention the finish line.

When everyone turned to see who was last, I stood there humiliated. This time my answers to the questions, not my lunch ticket, exposed me as a *have not*. Until then I had no idea how underprivileged I was. I thought I was doing well. However, even though my ethnicity, gender, and economic status of my family of origin were not under my control, they affected everything. I can't escape the facts of my life even with lunch money and a refrigerator full of groceries. I was born into last place or nearly last place. Even with the privileges I have now, I'll never be able to catch up with those who started ahead of me. That day, I discovered that even with my education and ability to think, fundamentally, I was still on society's and the American church's bottom of the pecking order. I was a bottom dweller.

JESUS' POVERTY

I suppose it is my background that causes me to be completely obsessed with Jesus' choice to live his birth, life, death, and resurrection underprivileged, at the bottom of society's pecking order. The apostle Paul speaks of this mystery in his second letter to the Corinthians, "You know the grace of our Lord Jesus Christ, that though he was rich, yet for your sake he became poor, so that you through his poverty might become rich" (8:9). What person, let alone God, in their right mind does this?

In loving obedience Jesus chose to leave his home in paradise, where he was cherished, known, and adored. He traded absolute shalom-filled power in exchange for slavery, becoming a nobody in the eyes of those he created. From paradise he willingly journeyed down, down, down into the dark but warm cave of his mother's womb. Jesus, divine and human both, nascent as a helpless babe. On his journey downward, he shed the privileges of divinity and became completely dependent on a human being. The first time our God opened his eyes, he gazed into the face of his mother. Had Mary not been able to feed him from her own body, Jesus would have perished.

Holy vulnerability.

Our God, the King of the universe and all worlds and possible worlds unimaginably beyond, chose to emerge as a pauper to two penniless parents on the outposts of society. When Jesus was circumcised, Mama Mary couldn't even afford to offer a little lamb as a burnt offering, as the Mosaic law required her to do in the temple on the family's behalf. Instead, she was only able to offer two turtle doves—the offering of the poor.

Not too long after Jesus' birth in a cave in Bethlehem—because there was not even room for God to be born—and after he was presented at the temple and circumcised in Jerusalem, he became a refugee in Egypt along with his parents. The Jewish superpower of the region, King Herod, was trying to kill him. Because even as a destitute baby, Jesus' presence was a threat to the most powerful in the world. And so our God knows what it is like to hastily leave everything, the comforts of life, to flee for his life into the arms of unfamiliarity and uncertainty and hostility. Either he remembered the refugee journey because of his divinity, or the oft-told stories Mary and Joseph shared with him over the years were forever tattooed on his heart. God identifies with refugees because he was one.

There is little security in being a refugee. The status and humanity of refugees, including refugee children, depends entirely on the goodwill and patience of the governments and peoples in the areas they flee to. It is easy to unsee them. Easy to divest ourselves of any responsibility for them. Easy to profoundly harm them.

After Joseph, Mary, and Jesus spent time on heightened alert as refugees in Egypt, they returned to their homeland. They could only return because the threat of execution and violence had temporarily passed. They settled in Nazareth. There Jesus grew up in obscurity, faithfully loving the Father and his neighbors as himself. It is in obscurity and lowliness among the Roman oppressors that Jesus grew in wisdom and stature. Carlo Carretto describes Nazareth as "the lowest place: the place of the poor, the unknown, of those who didn't count, of the mass of workers, of men subjected to work's grim demands just for a scrap of bread."

Like millions before and after him, Jesus, along with his parents, understood what it was like to toil for a scrap of daily bread. On days when he wasn't sure about where a meal was coming from when his cupboard was empty, I imagine that he might go to the outskirts of his town and pray, all alone—as he did when he was older. In communion with his Father and in his humanity, he learned to see.

He saw how our heavenly Father abundantly provided for the birds of the air and lavishly dressed the wildflowers growing in the fields about him. If our heavenly Father provided for the crows and sparrows, Jesus was convinced that God the Father would provide for him and any person who asked for something to eat and something to wear for protection against the elements, which could very well be brutal. Like the Israelites, day in day out Jesus had to learn to trust God the Father for manna in his earthly wilderness. Later on, Jesus would put two and two together and turn around and tell his disciples that he is the "bread of life" and that they must daily feed on him for existence.

Jesus, our God in the flesh and creation's royalty, lived at the bottom of society's barrel and grew up on the wrong side of the tracks. He who was independent of any mortal not only willingly chose to depend on his mother and father but also on the graciousness of other human beings. During his earthly ministry, he relied on the financial and practical support of women and others to sustain his ministry. When he was thirsty, he sat down and asked the woman at the well, whom the Eastern Orthodox and Eastern Catholics tell us is named Photini, for a drink. Saint Photini, a Samaritan woman, someone on the lowest rungs of her society, refreshed Jesus by giving him a drink of water. Jesus didn't discriminate in his dependence.

And he relied on others in his death.

Had it not been for Nicodemus and the generosity of Joseph of Arimathea, Jesus wouldn't even have had a proper burial. If the Romans had anything to do with his burial, Jesus' body would've remained on the cross decaying—a feast for crows. It is likely he would've been buried far outside the city in the area designated for executed criminals—a burial place of dishonor. Charles de Foucauld rightly observed, "Jesus has so diligently searched for the lowest place that it would be very difficult for anyone to tear it from him."

Yes, Jesus worked by the sweat of his brow for a few scraps of bread amid Roman occupation and oppression. Some days he knew hunger. But he also knew the poverty of relationships, a poverty that many of us know well. At one point early on, his own family thought he was sick in the head, out of his mind, because he was going around acting like the Messiah. Jesus, too, experienced familial dysfunction. And he knows what it is like to be harmed, to be stabbed in the back by those who are supposed to be his friends. In the upper room it was Judas. In the Garden of Gethsemane it was the rest of the disciples. During his trial it was Peter. Today we are the ones who betray him.

At the end of his life, in his final hours, his closest friends, the ones he had continually laid his life down for and would give up his life for, were profoundly unreliable and betrayed him. What poverty, what loneliness and pain he must've experienced!

Jesus lived unwelcomed and uninvited and misunderstood. Mistreated, despised, and degraded. John tells us, "He came to that which was his own, but his own did not receive him" (John 1:11). How crushing and exhausting to not be received by those who are supposed to be your people.

And yet in the midst of his volitional poverty during his life and death on earth, we see he learned humility—to completely depend on God and also on others. He had to. After all he suffered because of what he gave up to become fully human (while being fully God), he continues to wash the feet of his friends and enemies alike. Jesus, the God of the universe, rich as he is in every conceivable and inconceivable manner, washes my feet. And your feet. Even now, no place is too low for Jesus to stoop in order to serve others.

Behold the humility of God.

HESED

At our current church, our senior pastor, Russ, told us that the Jewish concept of *tikkun olam* means "world repair." Jewish theology teaches us repair of the world flows from God's *hesed* or "loyal lovingkindness." When we see and experience God's *hesed* in and about us, it is impossible to remain the same. *Hesed*, God's loyal lovingkindness, changes everything it comes into contact with. It changes us. And it leads us to repentance. Little by little, God's kindness transforms us from people whose natural inclination it is to creatively hate God and our neighbors to those who embody kindness. As *hesed* works itself out in and through us, the world repairs. Even in our poverty, that which brings us low and humbles us, *hesed* turns us into repairers of the world. It was true in Jesus' life and is true in ours. With God, we become healers and repairers of the broken even as we ourselves are being healed and repaired. God uses us to make all things new.

On my bad days, when I'm all twisted inside, I feel like *hesed* is really the only thing I have going for me. However, on these bad days, none of my poverty that fosters camaraderie with Jesus, and whatever lowliness has come of it, feels like a gift or *hesed*. I feel accursed like God loves those who have a relative life of ease much more than he loves me.

If kindness were the currency in this world, I'd be rich. But it isn't. So, I am not. These thoughts reverberated through my mind as I fled to my hotel room at a conference far from home. It all started with a look. One I am quite familiar with—a look full of ambition. I've seen it more times than I care to remember. It's the look of eyes scanning the crowd. Evaluating eyes. Up and down and all around eyes ricocheting in every direction in an effort to determine whether or not I am worthy. They're the eyes of a soul trying to figure out where I land in life's pecking order.

Soon enough, the body moves in the eyes' direction and toward the chosen one. It's not me but the one they've identified as having the most social or economic capital. I see them sidle up to the person, fawning and courting favor in their hunger for glory—in a hunger to fit in. I know the hunger. It's the hunger for glory and acceptance every one of us has.

I stood there weeping in my insides, awash in the little tears that pooled inside my soul. I blink hard trying not to let my tears escape. If my tears crest, like flood waters over the riverbank, I'll be swept away. My eyes dart to and fro. I need an escape route. I fear a well-meaning person catching me teary-eyed and asking, "What's wrong?"

I snake through the crowd. I am at the hors d'oeuvres table. It's close to the exit. I grab a napkin there. Blow my nose. Tears leak. I dab my eyes. If anyone happens to be paying attention I hope they mistake my nose-blowing and eye-dabbing for allergies. I've absolutely got to make a fast getaway.

Now, I'm out the door, race-walking to the restroom. I pick up the pace. I can feel a new stream of tears, the water table of my soul, rising to the surface. I dive inside and find the nearest stall.

I lean against the door, stifling my sobs so I can break down in silence. I wonder if maybe this person's estimation of me is right. Maybe I really am and ever will be just a nobody. *A Have-Not.* My life, inconsequential. I start berating myself for all I am not. Instead of sophisticated, I am simple—so I've been told. Instead of sassy and sarcastic, kind. Instead of social and economic capital and networks in the "right" Christian circles, all sorts of poverty are mine by way of birth. Any riches I might have don't count here, only in the kingdom come. Even here in this environment, a place where it's supposed to be a level playing field because we are Christians, I am still a pauper. Low on the pecking order. What good is *hesed* here?

I should call Shawn. The experience is poisoning me. I need to talk through this. Perhaps it has to do with culture and class. I can function in the middle class register, but maybe being formed in poverty, I never quite make it. I don't have the necessary sophistication or *je ne sais quoi*. "You can't escape your class," I've heard. Maybe I *should* stay in my place.

I grab my phone. But then I remember he's in class. Soon he will wrap up, dismiss his students, and head off to pick up our daughters after school. "Hi, this is Shawn, I can't take your call right now. But leave your name, a message, and a phone number, and I'll call you back as soon as I can." I hang up.

Once again, Shawn is juggling his heavy workload and the girls' schedules so I can be away for several days. He sacrifices so I can flourish. He willingly impoverishes himself of his agenda and free time for my welfare and the welfare of our daughters. Shawn is full of God's *hesed* expressing itself in self-sacrifice. For months, I've been nattering about all things related to the conference, dreaming about this day. We were both full of great expectations. If I unload on him, it'll break his heart. I'll have to manage alone.

I emerge from the stall now that I've finally stopped quaking. I am fairly certain I can hike back to my hotel room without falling apart in public. I make a run for it. Once inside, I hurl my book bag onto the floor and fling myself onto the bed. I lie there, face buried in the pillow, sobbing.

RE-MEMBRANCE

On my bed of tears, in my sadness and anxiety over never being quite enough, that feeling of never being among the chosen ones of this world began to quell. I grew still. I became "like a weaned child who no longer cries for its mother's milk. . . . [L]ike a weaned child is my soul within me" (Psalm 131:2 NLT).

Silence re-membered me by shouting truth.

I listened quietly.

Amid my tear-filled silence I vowed to myself that I would never do the same thing to another that for the thousandth time had been done to me. I wouldn't. However, in the silent stillness of the hotel room, reality materialized. I'd be fooling myself, engaging in self-deception, if I were to pretend that such behavior is below me. I, too, have done it before. I have.

Indeed, what I find quite disgusting and deplorable is that I too am tempted to use the same criteria used to judge me, to base the value of another person's life on the amount of money, influence, and power one possesses—on the person's vitality and contribution to society or to me. Worldly success. Utilitarianism.

We frequently show favoritism, preferring to hobnob with the rich and the affluent who have influence. We even sell our souls for political office and power. We instrumentalize one another, moving toward those who we believe can do something for us and away from those we believe have nothing to offer. How striking then it is when Jesus confronts us with the way of things, the way of the kingdom that is: "When you give a banquet, invite the poor, the crippled, the lame, the blind, and you will be blessed. Although they cannot repay you, you will be repaid at the resurrection of the righteous" (Luke 14:13-14). We say we value what Jesus values, but our lives and Christian subculture frequently preach a different message.

Jesus deemed the money-power-influence rubric we use to judge others, and our presumptions resulting from it, satanic. Indeed, the devil knows money, power, and influence are powerful lures that can easily become idols and lead to the corruption of our souls. Satan succumbed to these temptations himself. He is expert at using what he knows. Anytime we use the lenses of money, power, and social status to define another's value or our own, or to filter people out of our lives, we engage in godless devil's play. We dehumanize and do violence to others and traffic in the culture of death. The counterfeit trinity's deadly rubric has no place in the kingdom.

And yet the Christianized versions of devil's play do offer us glory. However, it's a twisted and diabolical glory. Short-lived and dangerous to our souls and that of others. Under the counterfeit trinity's spell, we elevate that which the world values instead of what God values. We dare not look to the counterfeit trinity for life and sustenance for manna. Its nourishment is no nourishment at all. It is malnourishment. Poison. Certain death.

> **The counterfeit trinity's deadly rubric has no place in the kingdom.**

My sustenance can never come from people's high or low opinions of me, from what I have or don't have, or from my social status. "I am the bread of life. Whoever comes to me will never go hungry, and whoever believes in me will never be thirsty," Jesus reminded me (John 6:35). That night, the words of 1 John 2:15-17 also functioned as an antidote to the counterfeit trinity's poison:

Don't love the world's ways. Don't love the world's goods. Love of the world squeezes out love for the Father. Practically everything that goes on in the world—wanting your own way, wanting everything for yourself, wanting to appear important—has nothing to do with the Father. It just isolates you from him. The world and all its wanting, wanting, wanting is on the way out—but whoever does what God wants is set for eternity. (*The Message*)

And so there in the hotel room, I committed again to living as Jesus lived and to his priorities for my life. I must live humbly and walk humbly with God. Accept the life given to me, his will for me instead of my own will for me, feed on him, and open myself to God's grace in my life. If I am to be like Jesus, a saint, I am going to have to walk away from what this world calls status and make the downward descent into kingdom status. You are too. It's the steep drop up.

A NEW WAY OF LIVING

Growing up and even into my adulthood, I despaired over the hand I was dealt. I often begged God to explain why the cards were stacked against me as a Hispanic-Latina woman born into a poor family that was plagued by the effects of mental illness. I used to despair a lot, but not as much anymore. Yes, there are instances like the hotel room. But I don't remain in self-pity for long stretches of time. On these occasions I am reminded that the gospel is especially good news for the poor, people on the lowest rungs of society, people like me and my family of origin. God gives grace to the humble. Though I am haunted by the effects of generational poverty, though I may have been born on the lowest rung in America, in many ways I am rich.

"Blessed are the poor in spirit: for theirs is the kingdom of heaven," Jesus tells us in Matthew 5:3 (KJV). People like me and my kind may be deemed poor and stupid and not worthy of a second glance. Animals to be caged. Not worthy to be anybody's teacher. But if your poverty and my poverty and deprivation (whatever form poverty takes in our lives) produce in us poverty of spirit, if our humiliations produce in us humility and dependence on God, then we shall be exalted now—in our lives with God—and in the life to come.

Rich.

> These are the ones I look on with favor:
> those who are humble and contrite in spirit,
> and who tremble at my word. (Isaiah 66:2)

When I remember what is true, instead of obsessing about nontruth or the hierarchies and idols associated with money, power, and fame, I can rejoice.

I am bidding farewell to worldly status. Along with Mary and Jesus, I am throwing my lot in with others who by the world's standards are disinherited and found at the bottom of all the hierarchies. Because I've found that God turns our hierarchies and our worldly values on their heads. It is only in our poverty and our intentional renunciation of worldly status seeking—in emptying ourselves of those ambitions—that we are ever open to being filled to the brim with grace. We cannot become full of God's life when we are chasing status, recognition, and honor from the world or the Christian culture—that only leads us to outer darkness. Like Jesus, we are to seek the lowest place and figure out exactly what that means for our particular lives. So, with Mary I marvel and sing:

> My soul magnifies the Lord,
> and my spirit rejoices in God my Savior,
> for he has looked on the humble estate of his servant.
> For behold, from now on all generations will call
> me blessed;
> for he who is mighty has done great things for me,
> and holy is his name.
> And his mercy is for those who fear him
> from generation to generation.

He has shown strength with his arm;
>he has scattered the proud in the thoughts of
>>their hearts;
he has brought down the mighty from their thrones
>and exalted those of humble estate;
he has filled the hungry with good things,
>and the rich he has sent away empty.
>>(Luke 1:46-53 ESV)

If we humble ourselves by seeking the lowest place, we will be exalted. God will fill those of us who are hungry and empty and poor with good things as we look to him to feed us and fill us.

3

All Flame

Prayer is an act of love; words are not needed.
Even if sickness distracts from thoughts, all
that is needed is the will to love.

SAINT TERESA OF ÁVILA

Abba Lot went to see Abba Joseph and said to him,
"Abba as far as I can I say my little office, I fast a little,
I pray and meditate, I live in peace and as far as I can,
I purify my thoughts. What else can I do?" Then the
old man stood up and stretched his hands towards
heaven. His fingers became like ten lamps of fire and
he said to him, "If you will, you can become all flame."

FROM THE DESERT FATHERS

Back in the day when there was prayer in school, there was slavery, lynching, and the genocide of the indigenous too. Our abuse, torture, and killing of others betray our prayerlessness and lack of love for sister and brother. God would rather have our life of prayer manifest itself in love for our neighbors, which demonstrates our love for him, over perfunctory prayer in school any day.

What is the essence of prayer? Prayer is beholding God whether as individuals or collectively. Gazing. There are innumerable ways, like lovers, to cup each other's faces, taking every detail in with galaxies of shared and unspoken intimacies. We behold one another's weeping and wailing. Other times in prayer we are alone with our thoughts and also with each other in a beautiful, vast silence. Or maybe in stunned silence. Or sharing in our *joie de vivre* or quarrels. We are free to use whatever modes of prayer and prayer aids are prescribed by the church.

So how is it then, and I've seen the picture, that a bunch of white-hooded, slit-eyed, family men behind impure white sheets, Ku Klux Klansmen, take a picture in a choir loft with a sign above them on the wall declaring "Jesus Saves"? Are these people of prayer, intimate with God, or wolves with the gall to not even wear sheep's clothing? Or are these wolves who smile for a picture under their peaked hoods inside the church and call out "Lord, Lord," but do not do what Jesus says? (see Matthew 7:21-23).

In daylight these were ordinary men who were the town's butcher, baker, candlestick maker, sheriff, and pastor. Under the cover of darkness they burn a cross and lynch an African American on a Saturday night, demonstrating anti-Christ behavior in word and in deed. Then on Sunday morning, they wake up, eat breakfast, and slide into the pew at church like nothing out of the ordinary happened. Except, the adrenalin of hate is still pumping in their veins during the Sunday service and flashbacks from the lynching the night before are flitting past their minds as they mouth the words to "Amazing Grace" or preach a sermon calling people to repentance.

Lord have mercy! How does that work?

Please, somebody, wax eloquent and tell me how those who can explain theology well, who can tell us where this and that Bible verse is found, who claim to pray to the God of the orphan and the widow can sexually, mentally, or physically abuse women and children? Talk about disassociation.

How can followers of Christ—those who claim to pray to the God of the stranger in our midst—justify the draconian immigration policies that allow treating those escaping poverty and violence and who flee to the United States to protect themselves and their families as subhuman? Agents of our US government kidnapped kids, locked them in cages, abused and molested them. Some were thought to be released to child traffickers never to be seen or heard from again. We as a nation are harming these precious children and families; our behavior is everything but pro-life. It is demonic and it causes some within our churches, and definitely many without, to do an about-face from the faith—to despise the church—because this is what those who claim to follow Jesus approve and justify.

How dare we approve of such policy and behavior and its consequences when Jesus says quite bluntly that "whoever causes one of these little ones who believe in me to sin, it would be better for him to have a great millstone fastened around his neck and to be drowned in the depth of the sea" (Matthew 18:6 ESV). Don't we sing the Bible song "Jesus Loves the Little Children" in our Sunday school classes? Well, does he or doesn't he love all the little children of the world? Those in the womb and those outside of the womb? And if Jesus does love them, then why don't we collectively love them in both word and *deed*? Love is never mere talk.

A good many of these little children and families are crying out to God for help and deliverance. Praying. Many of them are followers of Jesus. And even if they aren't, does it matter? A good many of us professing Christians in America who claim to pray and follow Jesus, who claim intimacy with God, are the ones handing them over to their death and destruction. We have blood on our hands and have had blood on our hands for a couple of hundred years (see Proverbs 24:11-12).

Love is never mere talk.

Frederick Douglass would have none of this so-called Christianity. Neither can I. Christianity lived out in mental abstraction, in our heads alone, isn't Christianity. Douglass nailed it when he declared, "I love the pure, peaceable, and impartial Christianity of Christ; I therefore hate the corrupt, slave-holding, women-whipping, cradle-plundering, partial and hypocritical Christianity of this land. Indeed, I can see no reason but the most deceitful one for calling the religion of this land Christianity." This type of Christianity is a stylized form of idol worship masquerading as Christianity. It's an angel of light Christianity, a wolf-in-sheep's-clothing Christianity. It's a bad marriage, where one spouse is a spouse in name only. First John 2:9-11 reveals to us core truths:

> Anyone who claims to be in the light
> but hates a brother or sister
> is still in the darkness.
> Anyone who loves their brother and sister

lives in the light,
and there is nothing in them
to make them stumble.
But anyone who hates a brother or sister
is in the darkness
and walks around in the darkness.
They do not know where they are going,
because the darkness has blinded them.

Any Christianity that justifies the hatred, mistreatment, or abuse of another is not the way of Jesus. It is heresy. It is offensive to God. The word is *anti-Christ*. It's good that Jesus has delayed his coming. For we have time to repent. Hateful postures, that is, ill-will toward our brothers and sisters through what we have done and left undone, will block our prayers. We cannot act in such a way and expect the shalom of God. We cannot act in such a way and claim to be in the light. If we do hate, I John tells us we are deceiving ourselves (and others) when we claim to be in the light, claiming to be enlightened.

LIVING PRAYERS: FASTING, PRAYER, AND ACTION

How then do we become the kind of people who are not akin to the Ku Klux Klansmen pastors and laypeople of our time but those who are living prayers and living answers to prayer for others? We begin first, I think, by praying for our enemies and moving in the direction of love. Jesus' teaching of loving our enemies and praying for those who persecute and mistreat us makes Christianity distinct (see Matthew 5:44).

It is often noted that we cannot hate someone we pray for. Eventually, we can't. We might not like them or have affable feelings toward them. We might start out hating them because of what they have done to us or others. But incrementally we get to the point where we don't wish them ill. We get to the point where we wouldn't say to them or think in our hearts, "Go to hell!" and mean it with every fiber of our being.

Grace is at work to transform us even if we have legitimate reasons for our hatred. It might take our whole lives to get there depending on how badly we've been abused and sinned against. That doesn't mean we put ourselves or our loved ones or the innocent in harm's way by being in the presence of those who have abused us or could abuse us or others. Depending on the level of transgression, maybe all we can whimper is, "I'm supposed to love my enemy. And so, I don't want to have hatred and ill-will toward them even though they deserve it. God help me!" God certainly turns his ear toward that whimper of a prayer.

> When Christ's life is pumping through our veins, when we feed on him, we become those who do not shrink back in fear over what others think.

When Christ's life is pumping through our veins, when we feed on him, we become those who do not shrink back in fear over what others think. We become those who are willing to take the public crucifixions of our reputations and who make the painful sacrifices of our time and money for Christ and his kingdom. This is the fruit of prayer.

Dallas Willard writes, "To understand Jesus' teachings, we must realize that deep in our orientations of our spirit we cannot have one posture toward God and a different one toward other people. We are a whole being, and our true character pervades everything we do." Nowhere in Scripture or in the teaching of the church do we find faith compartmentalized. Prayer energized by God's Holy Spirit action in our lives becomes a fast-moving, overflowing river whose forceful currents break down the dividing walls we have erected to compartmentalize our life in Christ and to separate us one from another. Willard goes on, "We cannot, for example, love God and hate human beings." No, we cannot!

Fasting and *prayer* are basic conduits of God's life in and through us. Throughout Scripture the two are paired together. Prayer and fasting are central to *kenōsis*. Traditionally, we fast by denying ourselves food. As we empty ourselves of food for a time and devote ourselves to prayer, we become full of God's life and sensitivities. It happens almost imperceptibly. As a child, I used to imagine, based on what I heard from radio and television preachers, that we fasted to more or less twist God's arm into giving us what we wanted. It was a magical formula: fast and God will give us what we want. To be clear: it doesn't work that way.

Fasting and prayer do fill us with power, but it's because through fasting and prayer we are attuned to the Spirit of God, to what God wants for us and the kingdom. Fasting and prayer form us into nimble and agile saints able to move at God's command and in concert with the heavenlies—far beyond what we can see or sense. Holiness. We become all flame as we surrender to God who is light of the world and in whom there is no darkness at all. We do not become God. No, but more like him. Bright lights. Remember when Moses spent time in communion with God on the mountain for forty days and nights and afterward? He came down with a face that shone so brightly that he eventually had to put a veil on his face (Exodus 34:29-35). Moses was all flame.

Fasting and prayer as individuals and together as a community allow us to become doers of the Word, not hearers only. Fasting and prayer together are a central way of emptying ourselves of that which is not Christlike that we might be full of the Holy Spirit. Consequently, we love and do what God loves and does. As a result, we possess a spectrum of powerful love for God and our neighbors because more and more we have the heart and mind of Christ (Philippians 2:2-5).

Amid Lent 2018 I had a strong sense of God's power when I took time away from food and social media to pray and to give of myself and possessions. Although I didn't know it at the time, fasting and praying during Lent prepared me to lead a public charge with co-organizers Michelle Warren and Nikki Toyama-Szeto against the "Zero-Tolerance Policy" the Trump Administration enacted in late spring 2018 where children were separated from their families when they sought asylum at the US-Mexico border. Christian women of all stripes came together to decry the inhumanity and brutality of that policy. A day or two after we led that charge, the president officially reversed it. Our prayer-soaked action, along with that of masses throughout the United States and world, had a concrete influence on the welfare of children and families. Prayer and prayerful action do. And so we continue to pray.

A LIFE OF PRAYER

True prayer brings about union with God. It results in a God-directed life and action. And in turn, union with our brothers and sisters. Clarity. Guidance. All sorts of healing. Changes in weather. Provision.

Prayer challenges the status quo of our individual and collective lives. This is certain: transformation springs from our union with God. If there is no transformation, can it be said there is true prayer or union? Transformation should spread throughout the church, society, and the world—if we are living out our prayers. To those who maintain prayer pretty much only changes us, I say "*Au contraire!*" or "Hogwash!" as some are wont to exclaim.

When I was sixteen I went on a mission trip to India. Back in the mid-1990s the trip cost about $4,000. That included the cost of the flight, transportation, and I cannot remember what else. Four thousand dollars is an astronomical amount of money for a poor person. My ten hours per week at McDonald's that spring wasn't going to cut it. I was leaving in June. When I enthusiastically told a visiting evangelist about my desire to go to India to share the gospel through film and my corresponding lack of funds or parental help in getting those funds, he said, "Maybe it's not God's will." I was deflated. I thought he would offer encouragement, suggestions, and some prayer. I went home and cried and cried in the room I shared with Abuelita. She was in the living room watching television, probably one of the smatterings of soap operas on Univision.

Then, I got down on my knees, reminded God of how he provided for everyone in Scripture and asked him to provide for me. I had the sense that the evangelist's word was not the word of God to me. I knew I was going to India, but not how I was going to get the money. Then the thought came to me, a thought not my own and never once one I considered or heard of before. "Get the phone book, start calling churches, tell them what you are doing, and ask for support." I did it even though I was scared to death to ask for money. Then, lo and behold, invitations rolled in for me to speak at Sunday morning and Sunday evening services about the trip.

In that short speaking-turned-into-preaching tour, I was lauded for my ten-minute convicting exposition of God's Word and for my testimony. They didn't mind that I was a teenage girl. Twelve country churches in the vicinity of Crawford County, Pennsylvania, supported me. It turns out that $4,000 wasn't too much for God and that the evangelist was wrong—though I am sure he was being practical, having the faith of an adult, not of a child, and not wanting me to get my hopes up.

I made it to India and fell in love with the Indian people and those on my team. We went to rural villages and worked with Indian residents to make an evangelistic movie. I was part of the film crew. But about halfway in I became sick with amoebic dysentery. I was miserable and weak. I was worried I would be sent home. One night we stayed in a small schoolhouse, probably two to three rooms. We had a team of thirty-two and so not all of us could squeeze inside. A few of us volunteered to stay outside in a small, enclosed courtyard.

There was one catch; the porch had no roof. That evening it poured. All I had was a sleeping bag. I was drenched. The others on the porch scampered inside and squeezed in. With no more room left inside, I laid my head and chest inside the doorway, the threshold. The rest of my body stuck out into the courtyard. It and my sleeping bag were sopping wet. But what could I do?

As it rained and I lay there in misery, it suddenly occurred to me that I could ask God to heal me. I had not one iota of desire to return home. All I wanted was to participate, to soak in India and its beautiful people. So, I asked God to heal me. I started naming and parading all the people in Scripture God had healed when they asked. I started in the Old Testament and continued through the New. I told him if he could do it for them, he could do it for me. What difference was there between them and me? I drifted off to sleep praying and to the sound of rain pummeling the roof. I woke up healed (and with a sopping wet sleeping bag and body)! Right away after I woke up, I knew I was healed. I couldn't believe it. God actually healed me.

Yet I can also name painful occasions when my prayers were not answered. Family or friends died without being healed in this life. A job is lost or a job goes unfound.

Even so, I'd hazard to guess that most of us expect little from God—at least those of us in the West. We've tamed and sanitized and desupernaturalized God, rendered him weak. At least we think and behave that way even if we wouldn't use those words to describe our posture. Or maybe we've been discouraged, had one too many disappointments, and so we cannot hope or believe anymore. If you're in that place, there's no condemnation. Only sympathy and empathy. I too have had times of darkness, of feeling lost, of living in the bleak wilderness, of wondering if God cares or even exists. It is a brutal experience.

But then I hear stories of God at work all around the world. Of miracles. Yes, there is evil, but we also live in a world full of goodness and kindness. These stories of communion with God and answered prayers are burning bushes, icons. They are reminders giving me hope because God is alive and well and at work even if I myself am in the dark and numb and lack understanding. Maybe our lives too can become a burning bush, an icon of answered prayer for another.

ICONS

I remember hearing a podcast in which Father Nick Louh, priest at St. John the Divine Greek Orthodox Church in Jacksonville, Florida, recounted a story about God's divine intervention. I followed up with Fr. Nick, and he graciously agreed to a phone conversation so I could confirm I had the story straight. In 2015 he and other members of his church set out on a humanitarian trip that led them to a village in Turkana County, Kenya.

As they approached the village, they could hear children crying out, "Mata! Mata!" Or Water! Water!" As they drew closer, the indigenous village priest came up to them and said, "It has not rained in our village in over a year. If this Jesus is so great, tell him to make it rain!" (Orthodox priests are easy to spot given their attire). Fr. Nick looked at him and then at a seven-year-old boy with a distended stomach. Inside he was thinking, *I'll pray but I am not sure it will happen.* As the group prayed, the indigenous priest walked around in a circle. It did not rain that night. They headed to the center of the village that morning, still no rain. "But soon after," Fr. Nick told me, "You could not have scripted this in a movie,"—"dark blue clouds came from the north, south, east, and west and descended on the village." It rained so hard that streams cut through the hard ground. People grabbed whatever they could to collect the water. "Everyone danced and shouted for joy, praising Christ." The rain came and there was a mass conversion of the village. Immediately, they chose to follow Jesus. "To this day," Fr. Nick concluded, "they are Orthodox Christians."

God answered the prayers of Fr. Nick's group and the needs of the villagers in Turkana County, Kenya. Fr. Nick tells me that it was "one of the top, one of the most significant" experiences in his life. And yet he returned home on a Sunday. Within the next week, his dad had a massive stroke and later died. Why did God answer Fr. Nick's prayers for the villagers and not for his dad? I don't know. But Fr. Nick emphasized to me, "We have to believe God hears our prayers. We're in a win-win situation with the Lord. Here on earth and in heaven."

These and countless other stories demonstrate that God is acting within history, in our particular lives, now and throughout the wide world. When and how he answers and chooses to act and whether we perceive God's actions or not, well, that too is mysterious.

PRAYER AND THE COMMUNION OF THE SAINTS

More mystery. If we consider the way things are, we realize our lives, including our faith in Christ, are never ours alone. We owe a great debt of gratitude to those who have walked before us: Protestants, Roman Catholics, and the Eastern Orthodox. Of course, we're indebted to the earliest Christians who were Jewish and thought of themselves as Jews. These are our forefathers and foremothers who handed down the faith to us. No matter how much we want to distance ourselves from one another, no matter how vehemently we disagree with this doctrine or that, we Christians are inextricably linked. There is no escaping our family resemblance. We belong to one another.

I think of those like my abuelita, my church family at Chapmanville Community Church in rural northwest Pennsylvania, and several other friends along the way who have loved me into resurrection. They are closest to me in generational proximity but are no longer here. Alas, the angels have borne them up to paradise where they are ablaze with life, forever feasting on the tree of life (Revelation 2:7). Here's a mystery I often think of: answers to prayers never stop with the death of the pray-ers, those who prayed. While the glorious ones feed on the tree of life, God is moved by his infinite love and their prayers to tend to me and form me here and now. The effects of their prayers travel throughout space and time remaining effectual for me and you until the end of time.

The book of Revelation tells us that the twenty-four elders and angelic beings, the cherubim, pour forth bowls full of incense, which are our collected prayers, the prayers of the saints (see Revelation 5:8; 8:4). Abuelita's collected prayers, and that of others, are encouraging God's life in me right now. Perhaps a way to think of it is that in and through their prayers, they pronounced a blessing over me that continues to bear fruit today. Indeed, our lives in Christ are the fruit of many prayers and much labor. The lives and prayers of the saints who have gone before are intertwined with ours. The great cloud of witnesses finds us right here at this moment. Our Eastern Orthodox and Roman Catholic brothers and sisters would insist the saints continue to pray for us even now. I suspect they're right.

> Our lives in Christ are the fruit of many prayers and much labor.

FORWARD MOVEMENT: PRAYING AND LIVING WITH POWER

Around my region I see lots of yard signs with the message "Pray to End Abortion." What might it look like on a wide scale if those prayers had legs? In addition to considering adoption, it would look like helping a single and struggling mother, who chooses to keep her baby, to get on her feet—with no strings attached. It means helping to provide food, housing, childcare, employment, and medical insurance. Education. It may very well be we are the ones to provide childcare. Maybe the mother and child will need to move in with us.

Moreover, it also means lobbying for and voting for public policies that make sure our most vulnerable children and families have easier access to medical care and education. If we truly pray to end abortion, our prayers will not merely enter the heavens by and by. We will count the cost. God will likely plan on using us, when possible, to be the answers to those prayers.

Father Evan Armatas, an Eastern Orthodox priest, had this to say about prayer and fasting, "To be living a spiritual life, you cannot simply pray. You are to be praying, fasting, and giving alms—all three." Lots of folks claim to pray and follow Jesus but commit atrocities without so much as a second thought. But true prayer intrudes into all aspects of our lives, upending the self-absorbed, hateful, and demonic influences of our lives. "If your prayer doesn't include fasting, acts of love, and charity, it can be dangerous because you lack love of neighbor. Fasting and prayer reorient us away from our own needs, create in us stability and strength in overcoming our own wants. . . . Prayer without fasting is not a biblical model," Father Armatas emphasizes.

In other words, if we are to be like Jesus and live like Jesus, we are to be people who fast and pray. These spiritual practices are directly connected to emptying ourselves of ourselves that we might be full of concrete love for God and for our neighbors, thereby serving them. "The kingdom of God is not a matter of talk but of power" (1 Corinthians 4:20). And so may we embody the prayer of Laura Jean Truman:

> God, there's hopeless apathy in my bones. Evil is too large. Our work is too small. When you came to save us, though, you didn't fight power with power. You came in smallness. Show us salvation in smallness. Help us to be faithful to the small, daily work of hope and justice. Amen.

4

Daily Returning Home

Bear fruits in keeping with repentance.

JOHN THE BAPTIST, LUKE 3:8 (ESV)

Truly I tell you, unless you change and become like little children, you will never enter the kingdom of heaven. Therefore, whoever takes the lowly position of this child is the greatest in the kingdom of heaven.

JESUS, MATTHEW 18:2-4

*M*etanoia, a definition: repentance: a change of heart. A turning. A change in course.

I am forty years old.

Slowly, I am becoming a child.

Saner and saner.

I pull my pants pockets inside out, shrug my shoulders, and tell God, "I got nothing."

No intrinsic goodness, no great abilities, no boots or bootstraps by which to pull myself up.

After giving birth to two little girls within three years, I finally started sleeping through the night a few years ago and managed to crawl to the local YMCA. Once, after a particularly intense workout, where sweat kept oozing forth from my pores, I decided to push myself further. I'd finish the workout with an intense bike ride.

I'm sitting there on the recumbent bike, pumping my legs, wishing my workout was over, and all of a sudden, I hear this guy, who some might dub a gym rat, say the following as loud as could be to his buddy: "You know what I did this morning? Same old, same old: I woke up, smoked some weed, and watched porn."

I sat there on my bike, pumping my legs, sweating, and thinking, *You've got to be kidding*. But I don't think he was. And then my thoughts immediately went to, "God, I thank you Shawn isn't like that. I don't have to worry about him smoking weed and watching porn. He loves me and the girls and. . . ." My avalanche of thoughts tumbled forth in that form until the Lord interrupted me. Again, I am still pumping my legs, with the din of gym life all around and the Lord was like, "Marlena, do you hear yourself? Do you hear what you are saying? You sound exactly like the Pharisee in the story of the Pharisee and the tax collector" (Luke 18:9-14). God turned the tables on me. And I was like, *Oh man, Lord, why do you have to play me like that?* To use a different metaphor: it's as if I were playing basketball, going up for a dunk, only to be stuffed, denied at the rim—by God. You know, the Lord talks to us in our own language and in ways we understand so we can "get" what he is trying to say.

Another way to say it: my brother-in-law, Chris, once quipped, "It smells as bad as a dumpster in August." Yes, that was the putrid smell emanating from my soul at the Y: a mountain of rancid garbage piled high and overflowing in the scorching, suffocating August heat. Odious. "Yucko!" as my girls like to say. Well, that was me!

You know, I don't like to think of myself as yucko or liken myself to an unrighteous Pharisee. I seldom think of myself as pharisaical. But who does? We are blind to our own sins and like to think that we are unbiased, righteous judges when it comes to the sins of others. But there at the YMCA my thoughts revealed wickedly pharisaic tendencies lodged inside my heart. Judgmentalism and superiority. Smugness. Self-righteousness. I came face-to-face with reality, with myself. I could easily be the man I was looking down upon. But within me dwelled something far worse. Who was the monster at that moment, the face of corrupted humanity? I'll give you a clue: it wasn't the pot-smoking, porn-watching guy.

The Lord was like, "Marlena, why don't you deal with the log in your own eye instead of pointing out the speck of sawdust in his?" He was gentle but firm. God didn't hold back. Comparatively speaking, I had a log in my eye, and "that guy" whose name I don't know but God does had a little irritant in his. It was going to take much more work, much more labor, to cut down the tree and excise what was protruding from my eye. Walking around with a log in my eye? I'm definitely dangerous and function as a menace to society. I can knock people out when I swivel my head this way and that. I can identify with the African American spiritual that begs me to remember to examine myself most of all:

It's me, it's me, O Lord,

Standin' in the need of prayer;

It's me, it's me, O Lord,

Standin' in the need of prayer;

Not my brother, not my sister,

But it's me O Lord,

Not the stranger, not my neighbor,

But it's me, O Lord,

Standing in the need of prayer.

So right then and there, as I was riding the stationary bike in an effort to get my body in shape, God showed me my soul was out of shape. Right there, after seeing myself for who I was and confessing to God who I was, I asked him to forgive me and change me and cleanse me deep within from my odious ways. I also prayed for the guy I initially found so repulsive. Maybe I should've begged him to pray for me! My hidden sins of pride and superiority were far worse than his. Lord Jesus Christ, Son of the living God, have mercy on me, a sinner!

I have learned that this sin has surfaced in another pernicious form. It is a lack of love for professing Christians who are giving Jesus a bad name and actively harming others. Whether I encounter them in person, hear about their fall from grace, or observe how they are oppressing the poor and marginalized through bad theology, politics, and practice, these are the hardest for me to love in my heart.

I'll go a step further. I often, though not always, associate them with a particular powerful stream of Christianity in our country. I hear its name and cringe. My visceral reaction is an internal eye roll. In my mind they are: ignorant, hypocrites, self-righteous, banal, shallow, lost, legalistic, anti-intellectual, lovers of litmus tests, greedy, oppressive, abusers of power, antipoor and marginalized, inhospitable to women, bullies, and on and on and on. These are the building blocks of my prejudices, of the bias in my heart, of smug superiority and pride. I can only see them amorphous and slack-jawed in their sins, flaws, weaknesses, and banalities. I don't have an eye for their goodness, and I don't even afford them the chance of being good.

In my life it's the same pharisaic tendency with a different object: "Dear God, I thank you that I am not _____." Essentially, I am thinking, *I am way too enlightened*. I am so tempted to right the wrongs in them—which is exactly what they attempt to do to other professing Christians and unbelievers. What travesties are found within me.

Not that denomination nor those a part of it,
But it's me, O Lord,
Standin' in the need of prayer;
It's me, it's me, O Lord,
Standin' in the need of prayer;

Part of the reason that self-righteousness, pride, and sins like envy and a lack of gratitude are so deadly is because they are prevalent within us but often not readily evident to us or to others. They lurk and strike when we are unaware and cause real-world harm and destruction to our own souls, to others, and in the world. Satan, the beautiful angel, was hurled out of heaven because of such sins. No wonder C. S. Lewis is right in saying that "a cold self-righteous prig who goes regularly to church may be far nearer to hell than a prostitute." If I let self-righteous judgmentalism run wild, I might find myself on the road to hell.

How beautiful and brilliant we can appear to ourselves and to others, but how far away we can be from God. Lord, have mercy! Jesus, save me from the flames licking at my feet!

The need, my need, for repentance isn't theoretical or a notion conjured up by an institutional church to shame us and keep us guilt-ridden under its thumb. The need to repent is not a false narrative that needs to be deconstructed. Whether we are an individual, family group, organization, church, or nation, it does us no good to ignore our sins or dismiss the notion of sin as antiquated, outdated, and out of step with the modern world. John the Baptist is still calling out to us, to me, "Repent . . . for the Kingdom of Heaven is near!" (Matthew 3:2 NLT). Repentance is a life-and-death matter. Repentance is the pathway to Christ, the kingdom.

> **Repentance is the pathway to Christ, the kingdom.**

HOME

Concerning repentance, Father Alexander Schmemann writes:

> It is easy indeed to confess that I have not fasted on prescribed days, or missed my prayers, or become angry. It is quite a different thing, however, to realize suddenly that I have defiled and lost my spiritual beauty, that I am far away from my real home, my real life, and that something precious and pure and beautiful has been hopelessly broken in the very texture of my existence. Yet this, and only this, is repentance, and therefore it is also a deep desire to return, to go back, to recover that lost home.

In the midst of having these thoughts and feelings about other people, I talk myself down. As Schmemann highlights, I realize "I have defiled and lost my spiritual beauty, that I am far away from my real home, my life." I've learned through practice to take the thoughts captive. I remind myself of the lovely, godly people I know in these churches. People whose lives are clearly Christlike. Yes, Christ is found in places and people not to my liking. My part in repentance is to stop the mental caricatures and dehumanization. The misrepresentations. Distortions. I have to stop despising them in my heart and like Eugene Peterson, begin "recycling my swords into plowshares."

Eventually, after much practice and purification from my sins, I will be transformed and return to spiritual beauty. One day, I will rarely have these thoughts or not at all.

To be sure, all this doesn't let them off the hook for wicked behavior. And if particular people or institutions are abusing and harming people, I need to speak up and act. And I have. I've been a whistleblower and have endured the blows and beatings and real-world financial harm and loss of community and excommunication that follows when the weak ones call the powerful out for their abuses of the weak.

Even so, I cannot opt out of loving those who are enemies to me and others. I am to love my enemies. But the pharisaism in me reminds me that I too am on the hook for the same type of behavior even if it is hidden in my heart. I will have to give an account for every thought, word, and deed. This is a life-and-death matter.

In repentance I turn my face back and lock eyes with Jesus. I stop looking at myself and others. My life then moves in the direction of my gaze. Toward Jesus. I leave the far country to run headlong into God's embrace. Home. I make my way toward wholeness by absorbing all that is good, true, and beautiful. It is only in beholding the face of Christ—doing whatever it takes to consciously keep my eyes on Jesus (see Hebrews 12:1-2)—that I know who I am, where I am, and whose I am. Jesus' face, his presence, is home. It's only in beholding the face of Christ that I enter deeper into reality.

Whenever I sin or allow sin to have its way with me, I turn against God, others, and creation. I ingest poison. Sin is turning away from the face of God. In my turning away and ingestion of poison, I turn my face away from the face of Christ and his presence. I leave paradise to embrace chaos.

God's life in me does not support my old ways, my old away from home ways of knowing, being, and doing. And so, I have a choice. Will I cooperate with God in emptying myself of my godless ways of knowing, being, and doing? *Kenōsis* through repentance?

God asks me to change course, to change direction and move toward life, toward re-creation into newness. Will I continue being saved? The choice is a daily and, depending on the struggle, a momentary reorientation toward him. God leaves the decision up to me, but knowing what I know about God and about what is good, for God is good, surrender or *kenōsis* is my only recourse. Repentance is to be the texture and rhythm of my life. If I choose to go my own way in the thousand tiny decisions, thoughts, and behaviors that make up my life, I deal death blows to everyone and everything around me, including myself.

Lack of repentance leads to a fantasy life, a fantasy existence.

But God calls me to reality.

God calls me home.

VIGILANCE AND CONFESSION

It can be hard to become a child. It is hard to be born again and go home when we've become so familiar with the far country and have built a home of wood, hay, or stubble there. We become expatriates comfortable in our filth. Many conversions after our initial conversion are necessary even if, like Nicodemus, we fancy ourselves well-educated in kingdom ways and means. When Jesus shows up unexpectedly, in one of his many advents throughout our lives, we discover we are hard of heart, slow to see and understand. We hear Jesus' words to Nicodemus coming to us, "You are Israel's teacher . . . and do you not understand these things?" (John 3:10).

I am Nicodemus.

Commenting on the theme of repentance in Saint John Climacus's "Ladder of Divine Ascent," Vassilios Papavasiliou writes, Repentance is "a critical awareness and a sure watch over oneself. . . . We ought to be on our guard, in case our conscience has stopped troubling us, not so much because of it being clear but because of it being immersed in sin."

In other words, we keep watch because it is possible for our conscience to be seared, deadened. At the same time, we are not to be unhealthily obsessed with our sins, rehearsing them to ourselves day and night and tumbling into despair as Judas did. Confession is not to be an unhealthy sadomasochistic practice, a hyperfocus on sin, a way of cutting ourselves. There's no need to pull a Martin Luther and climb the staircases of the Scala Sancta on our knees. We can go wrong in two directions—obsessing over all that is wrong about us and all of our sins or quickly dismissing the ways in which we turn away from Christ and toward death and destruction. Just because there is a possibility of going wrong in one way or another doesn't mean we abandon our efforts. We must keep vigil. Stay alert.

I am hereby protesting the Protestant Reformation's removal of the sacrament of confession. Protestant protests went too far. There's no doubt the medieval Roman Catholic Church needed reforming. And much good came out of the Reformation. However, in their zeal for reformation that turned revolution, our reforming brothers and sisters toppled many different means of grace. Should we name some of our early Protestant brothers and sisters "means-of-grace-oclasts?" Or do we consider these family members inerrant or authoritative in all matters for faith and life?

In confession, awareness is the first step toward freedom. It is one thing to name our sins to ourselves and to God. That is part of confession. There is no getting out of naming our sins. Naming our sins allows us to come face-to-face with who we are at this moment. But the sacrament of confession involves confessing our sins to a representative of Christ's church and receiving absolution. Confession in this traditional sense is of paramount importance. There is something mysteriously transformative in hearing the words of absolution: "In the name of Jesus Christ, you are forgiven."

Pastors, priests, nuns, and monks whose lives, not titles, demonstrate they walk closely with Christ can serve as our confessors. They can serve as our spiritual mothers and fathers. God forbid we be led astray by a kind, listening ear who knows little about life in Christ or by a scoundrel in clerical garb.

Interestingly enough, we can turn to Alcoholics Anonymous's twelve steps to learn the steps of repentance in their simplicity. I'll highlight steps 5-10 here:

5. Admitted to God, to ourselves, and to another human being the exact nature of our wrongs.

6. Were entirely ready to have God remove all these defects of character.

7. Humbly asked him to remove our shortcomings.

8. Made a list of all persons we had harmed and became willing to make amends to them all.

9. Made direct amends to such people wherever possible, except when to do so would injure them or others.

10. Continued to take personal inventory and when we were wrong promptly admitted it.

Steps 8 and 9 make it clear that repentance moves from remorse to action.

Doctor Luke uses the story of a wealthy tax collector, Zacchaeus, a sort of first-century Palestinian scrooge, to teach us about repentance (Luke 19). Basically, AA's steps are the steps of repentance. This short charlatan of a man had no qualms about using strong-arm tactics to extort money from his people. And yet in the end Zacchaeus the reprobate embodies repentance, demonstrating to all the world for all time the true nature of repentance. Repentance moves beyond remorse for our sins.

But, first, let's back up. I have a hunch that Zacchaeus's conscience began bothering him long before he sat perched atop a branch of the sycamore tree to get a glimpse of Jesus. I imagine Zacchaeus was conflicted. He was aware that he was doing wrong; his conscience wouldn't leave him alone. But he didn't know how to make right his wrongs or if he even had the moral courage and wherewithal to make it right. He reveled in his money and in the power and importance it brought in spite of his short stature. He liked having the finest seats at first-century events and, when he could make it, sitting courtside at the Hippodrome in Jerusalem for a chariot race. Tax collecting was a lucrative job providing him with fine clothes and rich foods and the fear-filled respect he garnered, even if it meant he resorted to violence to get his money, was a traitor, and hated by his fellow Jews.

Every spring, like a hawk, I keep careful watch of the blossoms on my friends, the trees. Whether it's gazing out my window or on a stroll down the driveway or walkway, I keep an eye on them. I do what I can to not let them out of my sight. I notice them tiny, just coming to life. Every day a little bigger. The leaves are infants, then toddlers in their vernal equinox. And then one day, maybe even within the span of a couple of hours, after I go to work or run errands or pick up the girls from school or forget to pay attention, they burst forth in their glory—surprising me every time. For once I wish I could just sit there, spellbound, watching it all unfold without interruption or a care in the world. But God sees it and enjoys it. And I can enjoy God enjoying it.

Like my precious little spring blossoms, it is impossible to know the initial moment when any one of us begins turning, making even the slightest pivot, toward repentance, toward wakefulness, toward God. We aren't fully aware of it. And yet that turning eventually becomes evident in our new thoughts and actions. Transformation begins. We are full of surprises for ourselves and others. Steeped in grandeur.

Maybe, just maybe, before the sycamore tree, Zacchaeus made a pilgrimage to the Judean wilderness to hear John the Baptist preach. Who knows if he was contemplating baptism. Maybe he was even baptized. In Luke 3 we hear John booming, "Produce fruit in keeping with repentance" (v. 8). When the crowd asked what it meant to produce fruit in keeping with repentance, John gave them specific instructions according to their jobs and stations in life (vv. 10-14). Tax collectors were in the crowd.

Perhaps Zacchaeus elbowed and shoved his way up to the front to hear John, the rising religious rock star. Tradition holds that Al-Maghtas is "Bethany beyond the Jordan," the locale of John the Baptist's ministry and the site of Jesus' baptism. There is a possibility that Zacchaeus was among the group of tax collectors who asked John what they should do to evidence their repentance. Al-Maghtas or "Bethany beyond the Jordan" is only about six miles east of modern-day Jericho. If Zacchaeus was present, he would've heard John say, "Don't collect any more than you are required to" (v. 13). Even if Zacchaeus wasn't present that day, surely he heard about John's teaching from other tax collectors in the area. *Don't collect any more than you are required to?* he may have muttered to himself. *How the hell am I supposed to make a living then?* he may have wondered. Such colorful language, that Zacchaeus.

Still, he couldn't shake this feeling of alienation. An alienation that he himself cultivated. An alienation from shalom— from all that is good. He alienated others through his death-dealing posture, words, and actions. People hated him, and he didn't like himself much either. No amount of money could change that.

Suppose Zacchaeus received word that Jesus brought a tax collector, a man by the name of Matthew, a man like Zacchaeus, into his inner circle. Maybe he heard of Jesus hanging out with tax collectors and other outcasts like himself. Maybe he wondered, *Could it be really true that a holy teacher, a miracle worker who claimed to be the Messiah, and who others believed to be the Messiah would draw close and befriend a tax collector like me?* Zacchaeus had to find out. He had to see Jesus for himself. When he heard Jesus was traveling through Jericho, he had his chance. He'd do anything to see Jesus, even clamber up a sycamore tree. The tree quickly became a window to heaven, a holy place for Zacchaeus, a pillar of remembrance for him and for us.

Imagine Zacchaeus's surprise when he looked down to see Jesus stop right under his tree. He looked down at God looking up at him. God in the flesh of a first-century Palestinian peasant face. He didn't see hatred or contempt in Jesus' face. He saw utter delight. Pure goodness. Twinkling eyes and laugh lines. And at that moment Zacchaeus felt his worth. Jesus liked him. And he liked Jesus. Immediately.

If we stop and take it all in, we see Christ's advent in Zacchaeus's life. Christ being born in Zacchaeus though he could see Jesus standing right in front of him. At that moment, *mysterious* isn't it? A turning. Then Jesus pulls out all stops and tells, doesn't ask, but tells Zacchaeus that he is going to stay at his house today (Luke 19:5). Jesus eating at his house was a profound gesture of intimacy and friendship. It is the most lavish gift Zacchaeus ever received. The Messiah at his house! This is how God rolls. Unexpected and lavish in grace. Grace is never stingy.

See Zacchaeus overjoyed and swimming in the presence of God. God's presence vanquished any nagging misgivings he had about the life of honesty and goodness, of the *narrow road*. He would change. He wanted to change. He felt himself changing! He would turn away from the life he knew—from the filth he was comfortable with. Just like that, he knew that the peace and joy he longed for was now possible. He could feel himself being filled. "Blessed are those who hunger and thirst for righteousness, for they will be filled," Jesus tells us all in Matthew 5:6. Because of the gratitude and goodness he experienced in the face of God, Zacchaeus chose to surrender his old ways of wheeling and dealing, that is, empty himself of his strategies for finding life *(kenōsis)*, in exchange for being filled with God's life and going God's ways.

And although his meeting with Jesus-full-of-grace-and-truth was quite unexpected, in an instant he knew that he would gladly sacrifice everything to be in God's inner sanctuary despite the murmuring of disbelief in the crowd who witnessed it: "Look, Lord! Here and now I give half of my possessions to the poor, and if I have cheated anybody out of anything, I will pay back four times the amount" (Luke 19:8). What he didn't know right away is that God would make Zacchaeus's life his inner sanctuary. That day Jesus embodied and exemplified John 14:23 for Zacchaeus and for anybody else standing around who happened to be paying attention: Jesus said, "Anyone who loves me will obey my teaching. My Father will love them, and we will come to them and make our home with them." Zacchaeus is no longer lost. God found him.

God wants to make our lives his inner sanctuary. His home.

Repentance is a turning, yes. We can also think of it as making room for God. When we repent, we give him a comfortable and comforting place in which to dwell. A home. We prepare a place for him. Our preparing a place for him happens to be a reflection of his preparing a place for us (see John 14:2-3). When we repent we are being hospitable to God. Is God comfortable in our lives, or is he claustrophobic because of the small space he is in? Does he have room to breathe and relax in our lives? Could he sabbath in us? Is God well in our lives or does the environment of our lives make him sick because of the many poisons within us?

> Repentance is a turning, yes. We can also think of it as making room for God.

A FEW MORE THOUGHTS ON REPENTANCE

"Forgiveness Sunday" is the last Sunday before Lent every year in the Eastern Orthodox Church. In Eastern Orthodox churches throughout the world, congregants seek forgiveness from one another. It is more than symbolic—even if one hasn't transgressed against another in the congregation. Father Alexander Schmemann explains, "It is true, that open enmity, personal hatred, real animosity may be absent from our life."

And then Father Schmemann brings us to our knees with the truth:

> But, the Church reveals to us that there are much subtler ways of offending Divine Love. These are indifference, selfishness, lack of interest in other people, of any real concern for them—in short, that wall which we usually erect around ourselves, thinking that by being "polite"

and "friendly" we fulfill God's commandments. The rite of forgiveness is so important precisely because it makes us realize—be it only for one minute—that our entire relationship to other men is wrong, makes us experience that encounter of one child of God with another, of one person created by God with another, makes us feel that mutual "recognition" which is so terribly lacking in our cold and dehumanized world.

He concludes:

On that unique evening . . . we are called to make a spiritual discovery: to taste of another mode of life and relationship with people, of life whose essence is love. We can discover that always and everywhere Christ, the Divine Love Himself, stands in the midst of us, transforming our mutual alienation into brotherhood. As I advance towards the other, as the other comes to me—we begin to realize that it is Christ Who brings us together by His love for both of us.

Repentance is not merely individual. Families, tribes, churches, states, and nations are to repent. All throughout Scripture we see God calling nations to repentance. Zephaniah 2 has a list of nations that God is judging for their lack of repentance. Repentance is collective because sin not only affects individuals; it is structural and systemic, affecting families, people groups, towns, cities, states, nations, and all of creation.

We see our collective sin against creation made manifest in the polluted streams, rivers, and oceans. We are poisoning the earth and ourselves. In Flint, Michigan, at the time of this writing, residents there still do not have clean water. It is full of lead.

Lead has terrible and irreversible effects on children's brains and bodies. We've privatized the gospel in America over the last two hundred years. But hopefully we are starting to figure out that our sin has structural, collective, and individual ramifications far beyond our imaginings in what is seen and what is unseen.

Do I want my life to be a blessing or a curse to those around me? Is my family a blessing or a curse to those around us—our neighbors, our neighborhood, our town, our church? Are our churches collective blessings or curses to those around us? Is our nation a blessing or a curse to our neighbors? Are we acting justly and bringing shalom? Our repentance and subsequent obedience will be the determining factor in whether or not we are a blessing or a curse.

One of the reasons why so many are scandalized by the church who claims to follow Jesus is because the church collectively does not do what it asks of its congregants. That is a curse. We turn on the news and hear of another church that has covered up sexual abuse, greed, and power plays. Another pastor or priest preaching one thing and living another. But even after incontrovertible evidence and testimony, the church leaders deny or dismiss wrongdoing.

Wouldn't it be phenomenal to see true communal repentance coming from those who have sinned against many instead of them covering their tails? That would be a blessing. Repentance means "turning," and turning turns away from sin and toward accepting the consequences of sin, come what may. Collectively, we might lose everything by admitting we are wrong and by facing the consequences and repenting, but then again we'd gain our collective soul and become a communal blessing. May we bear fruit in keeping with repentance.

5

Do You See What I See?

TRANSFIGURATION

I want to practice looking at people as though it were God looking at them—to be a mirror of God's loving gaze. This requires me to be truly present to whoever is in front of me.

DEBORAH A. SMITH

D o we see what God sees?

Every Sunday morning in the foyer or in the sanctuary, our eyes met. Paula's eyes, full of joy, twinkling even before she flashed her beautiful, jaw-dropping, million-dollar smile. Immediately she'd break into song, loudly singing my name, "Mar-le-na!" She had a strong, melodic baritone voice. Whether she slowly wound her way over, or it was me making a beeline to where she was sitting, we'd hug, and I'd say, "It is so good to see you." "It is good to be seen," she'd tell me. And then I'd remind her, "You know I love you." In her childlike trust and confidence, she offered, "I know you do."

Once she confided, "In school, someone called me 'Moose' because I am big-boned and tall. I felt ugly." "But Paula," I said, "You're one of the most beautiful people I know! Besides, your glasses are so fashionable, and I could never wear my hair as short as yours and look good. You look great." I gave her a peck on the cheek and no more was mentioned about ugliness. But I could sense those words spoken so long ago still hurt. But just as suddenly as the cloud had passed over her face, the sun came out again and she broke out into her famous and frequent rendition of "Supercalifragilisticexpialidocious," as popularized in the 1964 film *Mary Poppins*.

Most always she was full of joy. It was only one other time, a Wednesday night after we greeted one another with glee, that her eyes welled up with tears. "Oh Paula, what's wrong?" I asked in alarm. "Do you think God still loves me even though I forget?" she asked. "Of course, he does, Paula. Of course, he does!" I gave her a hug and a peck on the cheek. Her husband, Bill, patted her on the back in reassurance. "Good."

My dear Paula was seventy and dealing with early onset dementia. It was quickly progressing. That's why each time we met, I was deeply touched when she remembered my name. Every time she called "Marlena!" was a great gift.

A few hours after that encounter, I returned home. I couldn't stop thinking about Paula and told Shawn about what had happened—about her "Do you think God still loves me even though I forget?" question. "What do you think about us relating to God and God relating to us when our memory is failing?" I asked him. "What about when one's mind, like Paula's, isn't doing well?" He answered, "I don't think Jesus minds reintroducing himself to Paula over and over again." "Of course, he wouldn't!" I squealed. The thought of Jesus reintroducing himself to Paula and others with similar conditions over and over again sent me diving headlong into a sea of delight.

Whenever I saw Paula, I saw and experienced Jesus—Jesus welcoming me with joy. Jesus reintroducing himself to me over and over again. When I meet him, I have a hunch Jesus will welcome me, eyes full of joy and cheer, singing my name. At the time of this writing it's been about three months since Paula died from the effects of dementia and of a heart that simply wore out. Now she remembers everything and is full of pure joy in Christ's presence. I trust she remembers me.

IMMORTALS: FAME HERE, FAME THERE

For the most part, I don't like to watch movies over again. Usually it's one and done—unless I watch it several years or even a decade later. But I do have a penchant for rereading books, or portions of books, that I consider a gold mine of wisdom. I pore over them carefully—the way I try to read Scripture.

I have a bookshelf for my special friends, these books of mine. I nearly always haul a select few out as travel companions. At a retreat, in a plane, on a train, or in an automobile, I'm like a forty-niner panning for gold in rivers and streams the way they did during the 1849 California Gold Rush. One such gold mine of a book is C. S. Lewis's *The Great Divorce*. I relish the stories and rich imagery it contains. I read or listen to it every year. It has certainly formed me.

One of my favorite stories from the book is about Sarah Smith of Golders Green. The narrator, who I think of as Lewis, and his guide, Scottish writer and pastor George MacDonald, encounter a great parade in honor of a woman. He describes it like so:

> First came bright Spirits, not the Spirits of men, who danced and scattered flowers. Then, on the left and right, at each side of the forest avenue, came youthful shapes, boys upon one hand, and girls upon the other. If I could remember their singing and write down the notes, no man who read that score would ever grow sick or old. Between them went musicians: and after these a lady in whose honour all this was being done.

Lewis's best guess is that the woman being honored is astronomically famous. He inquires about her:

> "Is it? . . . is it?" I whispered to my guide. "Not at all," said he. "It's someone ye'll never have heard of. Her name on earth was Sarah Smith and she lived at Golders Green." "She seems to be . . . well, a person of particular importance?"

And here my friends, with the following answer, coming out of the mouth of George MacDonald, Lewis's guide, is where we strike pure gold and become filthy rich—if we can but comprehend its weight in the kingdom of God:

> Aye. She is one of the great ones. Ye have heard that fame in this country and fame on Earth are two quite different things . . . already there is joy enough in the little finger of a great saint such as yonder lady to waken all the dead things of the universe into life.

FAMOUS IN GOD'S EYES

I only included an excerpt from this passage in *The Great Divorce*. However, in context, we learn further that Sarah Smith of Golders Green, a never-heard-of person on earth from the backwater, invisible and unknown to the great swaths of humanity, with a name never mentioned in the papers, social media, or history books, is most famous in heaven. She is famous in the eyes of God and in the eyes of those who have eyes to see.

Her fame came by way of loving and serving everyone and everything about her—men, women, and children, and all of creation. Sarah Smith of Golders Green was practiced in emptying herself on behalf of others. *Kenōsis.*

While overlooked, underappreciated, and perhaps misunderstood on earth, God took note of every miniscule detail of her life. Her loving service flowed naturally from who she was becoming in God. Christ in her, the hope of glory, overflowed into the world. Everything and everyone touched by sanctification because of who she was becoming in Christ.

"Ye have heard that fame in this country and fame on Earth are two quite different things" and "already there is joy enough in the little finger of a great saint such as yonder lady to waken all the dead things of the universe into life."

Yes, pure gold!

With everything in me, I believe this is true!

The apostle Paul tells us of this incomparable and, I believe, joyful power that can bring dead things to life. It is a power that comes from God's life in us. It is power that "is the same as the mighty strength he exerted when he raised Christ from the dead and seated him at his right hand in the heavenly realms, far above all rule and authority, power and dominion, and every name that is invoked, not only in the present age but also in the one to come" (Ephesians 1:19-21).

But we have to be in a humble servant's position to experience that power. Only in such a position will we have eyes to see even a bit of that power at work in the world. No wonder Paul prayed that the Ephesians' eyes might be "enlightened," that is, opened, that they might "know" the hope God has called them to, their "glorious inheritance" as saints and the "incomparably great power" available to them in Christ Jesus (Ephesians 1:18-19). The same holds true for us. Our eyes have to be opened to see.

EATING DIRT

Sarah Smith's life was a life bowed down. When we bow or kneel, we are taking the position of a servant, expressing with our bodies our submission. And when we bow or kneel or fall prostrate, we are closer to our terrestrial origins: dirt, soil, mud, and muck. Humus—from whence comes the word *humility*.

Jesus bent low to the ground as he washed the disciples' dirt-stained, filth-ridden feet, rendering himself vulnerable to being kicked, pummeled, and injured by those who were now in a position of strength above him, by those he was serving. Humiliated. The posture of a servant is one of bent knees. Washing soiled feet. It is a close-to-the-earth, face-to-the-ground posture. Vulnerable. It is only in this lowly position, a servant's posture, that glory is revealed and that we have the possibility of glimpsing the grandeur and glory about us. We are able to truly see when we see the earth from below rather than from above.

But the sin-sick systems of this world insist that glory involves standing completely erect, as far away from the ground as possible. Capitulating to this, we falsely believe that glory comes when others toss themselves at our feet, bowing before us. How interesting it is that during Jesus' postbaptism temptation in the desert (Matthew 4), Satan urged Jesus to bow before him, to fall at his feet, to eat the dirt he stood upon. Satan, a created being, stood tall,

> We are able to truly see when we see the earth from below rather than from above.

chin up, nose in the air, high and mighty like others steeped in the perverted ways of this world who are nowhere close to the earth. His inflated head was in the clouds as he stood atop his self-made rickety Tower of Babel and tried to woo Jesus, his maker, into putting his nose to the sunbaked sand. Satan himself would never dream of bowing low before his Maker.

Pride removes us from our origins. It blinds us. We forget where we've come from—dust—even though we rehearse it at Lent with ashes on our foreheads and still hear it at some funerals: "From dust we came, and to dust we will return." The high and mighty of this world strut about with an air of swagger and security, accompanied by a groveling entourage and with access to places the poor and lowly will never have access to. "It is easier for a camel to go through the eye of a needle than for someone who is rich to enter the kingdom of God" (Matthew 19:24). But the poor and poor in spirit remain close to their origins, in a posture which puts them close to the earth—humus. And that breeds humility.

Worship is taking our proper creaturely posture before our Creator God and, consequently, our neighbors—the position of humility, the position of a servant. Maybe it's lying prostrate begging for divine mercy or in unfettered adoration of God. Maybe it's on our knees, exhausted by the relentless pressures of life or astounded by the beauty of God's handiwork. Maybe it is serving and seeking the flourishing of our local and global neighbors and the rest of the natural, created order.

Three times during his earthly tenure Jesus was elevated high above the earth: the transfiguration, his crucifixion, and his postresurrection ascension. And in each case God the Father lifted him up. Jesus did not rise of his own accord. It was not by his own strength nor by his own might. There was no "pulling himself up by his own bootstraps." He had long practiced *kenōsis*—freely making his will subservient to the Father's.

"Humble yourselves, therefore, under God's mighty hand, that he may lift you up in due time" (1 Peter 5:6). With these words Peter simply reflected upon what he had learned from Jesus: we don't raise ourselves away from the earth on our own; we wait for God to lift us up. Interesting in that it is in living things' close proximity to and deep rootedness in the ground where growth occurs. It's where we gain perspective, in the low places, in the dirt. That which is bent low rises in the glory of God—eventually and ultimately. Another mystery.

> That which is bent low rises in the glory of God.

THE GREAT ONES AMONG US

It all comes down to eyesight. I sit with this reality day in and day out as it makes its way deeper inside of me, as it forms me. I am slowly coming out of the darkness and into the light. Jesus is taking my hand and drawing me outside the village—into the desert where people are few and far between. Jesus gently puts his hand on my head, the way pastors and priests do as they bless. He asks me if I can see anything.

When we are coming out of the darkness, the light stings our eyes. We shield our eyes. For the longest time all I saw were shadow shapes, people walking about as trees—not people as they are—not people the way God sees them. But glory be, my vision is being restored (see Mark 8:22-25).

Have you ever encountered anyone so overwhelmingly brilliant that you are tempted to bow or curtsy before them like one would a queen or king? I have.

On any given Wednesday night, a ragtag group of us, ten at the most, sit in a holy huddle in our prayer meeting. Except, I doubt any objective onlooker would dub our huddle "holy." They'd probably call us "misfits" based on contemporary standards of success. There in our church's tiny chapel we circle around in chairs or on a pew to pray for each other, our church, our community, and the world. Always from six to seven p.m.— rain, snow, or shine—all throughout the year. Really the only time we cancel is when ice or snow makes driving too hazardous.

One day, after she was gone for two weeks, Lynn strolls down the hall in the church office. She serves as her own herald as she trumpets her arrival: "I'm baaack!" Pastor Russ and I bolt from our respective offices (when I worked at the church) to welcome her back with great fanfare. Upon seeing us, she is giddy, smiling from ear to ear. We heap praise left and right—trying to outdo one another in telling the truth to Lynn, about Lynn. We gush forth a Niagara Falls amount of "How on earth could we survive without you?" and "Our lives aren't the same when you are not around." Pastor Russ easily outdoes me in his antics of joy surrounding Lynn's return but not in sincerity nor sheer amount of joy. When it comes to those, we are neck and neck.

Lynn's pure, unadulterated glee upon her arrival back home to our church and over our reception of her is not to be forgotten. Pastor Russ and I agree that that's how we want to be welcomed, received, and loved. The thing is, Lynn has mild to moderate intellectual disability. Back in the day, the moniker given was "mental retardation." But she has taught us something essential to God's character: his way of loving and welcoming us, his way of rolling out the red carpet. She welcomes others in the way she expects to be welcomed. Both Pastor Russ and I could testify that Lynn is a "Sarah Smith," that there is enough power in her life to bring dead things to life. Christ in her has brought dead things in us to life.

Carolyn is also in our group. She is a gorgeous African American woman. At one time, she was a pharmacist. "I used to have lots of money" and "a nice car," she told me. "But now . . ." Her voice trails off.

If you knew fifty-year-old Carolyn at all, she might confide that she is self-conscious about her weight. She wants to lose weight. It is bad for her knees. Bad for her back. Bad for her self-esteem. She is thinking about bariatric surgery. "The side-effects from my medicines aren't helping any, either," she'd say. A decade ago, her bipolar flared—roared, actually. It quickly became evident she could no longer work as a pharmacist. The daily side-effects of her condition and of the medicines she takes for it attempt to rule her life like an iron fist.

Poverty stalks her.

Will she have enough money to fix her car, or should she use a huge portion of her monthly disability check to fix the raw sewage backing up in the basement? Or maybe she should use the check to pay for a doctor's visit because she severely injured her knee somehow and now needs a cane to get around. These are the common dilemmas of her life. She regularly robs Peter to pay Paul. And even then she might come up short when she tries to pay Paul. If you knew Carolyn, you can bet she won't volunteer this type of information easily. No, she won't. I know because we are friends and because I ask how she is *really* doing and if she needs anything.

If you think we only see Carolyn as her disease and her deprivations as a liability or a problem, you'd be dead wrong. Intelligent. Stalwart. A pillar. A lifeline. Ask our Wednesday night prayer group. Ask our pastors. Ask anyone in the church who knows her. She is a counselor and confidant, an encouragement, a shining star among us. A shining star in the universe. Great in God's sight. Whatever good she receives from any of us pales in comparison to the benevolence we receive from her.

When we haven't seen her for two weeks in a row at prayer meeting or in church, we'll text her. Call her. If need be, someone will stop by. We worry when she is absent. We're finally at peace when she gets back to us and tells us that she had a rough couple of weeks.

Around our circle of half folding chairs and half pews, Barb sits across from me most every time. Or maybe I sit across from her. Our dear Barb, or Barbie, as her daddy called her, is a young seventy-three and a ball of absolute sunshine. She tells me that she gets her gray-black hair set once a week. And her nails and toenails are always done up in some elegant color. Most of the time she has lipstick on and blush on her face. Barb is fastidious about such things. But one day as prayer meeting is starting, she tells us, "It's hard to know what my purpose is anymore."

She can no longer do the things she used to do—head committees and missions and outreach or serve in all the other capacities in which she used to serve. Parkinson's disease has slowed her down. It is progressively debilitating her. She has tremors. At times, her legs give out. Her eyesight is going bad. As a result, she might have to give up driving soon. "The one good thing about it," she jokes, "is I've lost a lot of weight. I get to buy a whole new wardrobe. For years I've been trying to lose weight. Now, it just comes off easy." I tell her that when I am her age, I want to be just like her, a sunshiny encourager, and also like Jean, who is sitting by her side.

Ahh, Jean! She is quiet and calm and very attentive to life and to the person right in front of her. She has a warm and soothing presence. She is a balm to my soul. In our little circle her prayers are brief and to the point. Not only does Jean intercede on behalf of others, but I quickly learned that she becomes the answer to her own and to our prayers. She visits shut-ins weekly. And she does things like collect money and clothing for kids who were left behind when Immigration and Customs Enforcement raided Corso's Flower and Garden nursery, which is about an hour away from where we live. When parents or guardians were hauled off to detention centers, children were initially left to themselves. Jean sprang into action to help them without any coercion from anybody else. That's Jean—bringing goodness into the world through her presence and action. She is a spry eighty-eight years old.

There are countless others before whom I would bow. Saints that I revere. I am inclined to bow because I see better. They have been there all along.

GOD LOOKS HAPPY AT ME

Several years ago my then three-year-old Valentina caught me staring at her. "Mommy, why are you looking at me like that?" She caught me off-guard. I didn't even know I was staring. "Because I love you and delight in you," I said. She must have caught my eyes glued on her, sparkling in delight. A moment later it occurred to me to further respond with, "God looks at you that way too." "You mean, God looks *happy* at me?" she earnestly inquired. "Yes!" I said. "God always looks happy at you," I emphasized. "Then I look happy at Jesus, at you, at Daddy, and sisters," she concluded. When she finished, I think she could see me beaming with even more happiness. I want my three daughters to know deep down that God loves them and delights in them—that God looks happy at them. Indeed, God looks happy at each one of us and welcomes us the way Lynn expects to be welcomed and received. God is like that.

Those in our little Wednesday night prayer group circle, they are good seers. They are God-seers. Not only do they see the reality of things, but they see the reality of who I am. I can look into their eyes, I can be in their presence, and know who I am. They mirror God's view of me. They look happy at me.

Those looking in at those in our prayer group (I didn't detail the beauty in the lives of Mary, who I call the "Overcomer," or Cathy or Michelle), those who don't know, might think we're a bunch of has-beens, that life has run out on us. Along with our two pastors they might notice atrophying hands, knees needing surgery, intellectual disability, a mind fading, poverty, anxiety, insecurities, and those fighting hopelessness. Externally, we might be fading away, but day by day we are being renewed—growing young—childlike in the kingdom (see 2 Corinthians 4:16). Each of these dear ones is close to the earth. These intercessors know their position before God and are waiting for him to lift them up in due time. Here in our little circle I see God up close; I see the life of Jesus at work in powerful ways.

"The eye is the lamp of the body. If your eyes are healthy, your whole body will be full of light. But if your eyes are unhealthy, your whole body will be full of darkness. If then the light within you is darkness, how great is that darkness!" (Matthew 6:22-23).

6

Our Teachers

MESSENGERS OF GRACE

*But many who are first will be last, and
many who are last will be first.*

MATTHEW 19:30

*The rich man shouted, "Father Abraham, have some pity!
Send Lazarus over here to dip the tip of his finger in water
and cool my tongue. I am in anguish in these flames."*

LUKE 16:24 NLT

I walked the streets of New York City only once before. I was on a spring break trip with my best friend Kim and her fiancé, Chad. We boarded the train in Philly. Slipped unnoticed through Trenton, New Jersey. After a two-hour ride we stepped off the train and headed straight to the Guggenheim Museum. At the end of the day we returned home—too tired to go anywhere else.

This time I flew from Dayton to Boston and then into JFK for a Q Ideas conference. One of Shawn's former students studying philosophy in New York fetched me at the airport, escorted me onto the subway, and walked blocks and blocks and blocks with me and with my luggage in tow. We then met his wife, also studying in New York—comparative religion—and our mutual friend, a painter. All four of us headed off, me with my carry-on sized luggage still in tow, searching for an affordable restaurant for our meager budgets.

On our way I noticed a huge commotion. I motioned for my friends to stop as hordes of people filed past us on the Manhattan sidewalk. I stood, gawking—holding up foot traffic. Right there in front of me, the NYPD was roughing up an African American man. A crowd of them surrounded him, poked and prodded him with their batons, and shoved him in an effort to get him to move from the storefront. He was in a fetal position. He wasn't permitted to sleep there.

He didn't budge.

Nor did he utter a word.

He wasn't blocking the entrance. He wasn't bothering anyone as far as I could tell. All he wanted, I think, was to sleep in a well-lit and safe place—the safest place being in the public eye. He could rest his back against the storefront. There he wouldn't have to worry about being mistreated, or so he thought. But others, maybe the store manager or clientele, considered him an eyesore. A nuisance.

When the others turned their eyes in the direction of my gaze and bore witness to what I saw, one quietly told me, "This happens all of the time. We've gotten used to it. Maybe we shouldn't be used to it. We want to do something but don't know what to do." I wondered what I could do. What were my options? What if they hurt him? Call 9-1-1? Call the police on the police? Try to step in, not quite 5'3" of my little Puerto-Rican self, who is clearly much bigger on the inside than I appear on the outside? I was paralyzed. Cut to the heart. This was back before people filmed such events. I had a flip phone still. "That's wrong," I said. "Wrong." We all agreed. We resumed our trek, in search of a restaurant. We kept walking. Now in silence.

As I walked away I wondered about what could be done and about what I should've done. Why are the most vulnerable among us, homeless minorities, treated with such contempt—not only by some members of the police force but by Christians like me? Why are folks homeless in the first place when we have enough empty houses to house them? All I know is I failed that man. Failed him. I should've tried to stop them. Whatever fueled my moral failure—be it confusion, fear, or resignation—whatever fueled my failure to love, I know this: I believed the lie that I could do nothing.

For indeed, Jesus comes to us in many disguises—including disguises for which we have no use. And then we lament with tears that God does not speak to us. I encountered Jesus being harassed and moved along. And like the disciples in the Garden of Gethsemane, I fled by walking away. Like the priest and Levite on the road to Jericho, I passed by on the other side. I encountered Lazarus at my gate and ignored his plight in exchange for my own self-preservation.

And it was night.

AN UNVEILING

When Shawn and I lived in Rochester, New York, we were the codirectors of our church's youth group. In addition, Shawn was in graduate school studying philosophy, and I was in seminary while also working full-time at a nonprofit. At nights we'd tumble into bed exhausted but content. In this context I became exceptionally disturbed after reading Matthew 25:31-46. These verses are a warning about the Final Judgment— *apocalypsis*, apocalypse, an unveiling or revealing.

Writer, author, and assistant rector Preston Yancey was the first person I heard who pointed out on Twitter that the last few years in our American society have been apocalyptic— they are revealing much in particular about who we Christians are despite what we say about who we are. Our actions speak volumes. They are louder than our words.

Matthew 25 is about the end of time as we know it. On that End Day, Jesus separates the righteous from the unrighteous the way a shepherd separates sheep from goats. At that moment you and I will find ourselves among the throngs of people from every era. Sappho and Cleopatra, Genghis Khan and Napoleon will be there. And there will be the greatest of saints there, most of them obscure and previously unknown to us and most of humankind.

Some will get the surprise of their lives when they find out that they are one of the great ones as their spirits are slowly transfigured while we all stand there watching and waiting. In this life they didn't think much of themselves or think about themselves much but sought to love God and neighbor with their whole beings with little earthly reward or recognition.

They are the Sarah Smiths of Golders Green. We'll turn to look into the sea-sized crowd from every tribe, tongue, and nation. Their presence will blind us with light because of the number of people all over being transfigured into shining stars of the universe right before our very eyes. Maybe we will be one of them. On that day much will be revealed—apocalypse. We will finally see ourselves and each other for who we are.

And we'll turn our gaze in the other direction and witness others morphing into hideousness as their insides are revealed, as C. S. Lewis described in his sermon turned book *The Weight of Glory*. Some of us will shriek in the horror of all horrors when we notice that we've become the hideousness we secretly gave into all along. The details of this unveiling have yet to be revealed. But we can mark Jesus' words. It will happen. It is happening even now. What we see now is apocalyptic foreshadowing.

LAZARUS AND THE RICH MAN

Some of the kings and queens transfigured into the brightest of lights at the end of all things will have been the Lazaruses of our world. And those who morph into hideousness may very well be the bright lights in the world's eyes and supposedly bright lights in the church. Those who called Jesus "Lord, Lord" but did not do what he said and who did many miracles in his name but were not known by him (see Matthew 7:21-23; 25:40-46). Indeed, it will be a conjoining of Matthew 25 and the story of Lazarus and the rich man in Luke 16:19-31 on the day to end all days.

Jesus tells the story of a certain rich man who had nothing really to worry about in this life. He had a nice first-century middle-class life with a spacious house—it had curb appeal and a walk-in closet full of all sorts of sandals made by expensive cobblers and name-brand robes made by the finest tailors. He even had enough leftover food scraps to give to his dogs. Lazarus, on the other hand, was a poor beggar who stationed himself right at the rich man's gate. From the rich man's perspective the sucker Lazarus had the gall to loiter about the gate of his glorious estate every day.

For Lazarus's part, all he longed for, all he really wanted were a few measly table scraps from the rich man's table. Day in and day out he sat at the rich man's gate with dogs licking at his open wounds. You see, he couldn't earn money to buy food, nor could he afford any health care. At least the dogs had compassion on him even if no one else did. Blessed be the dogs.

The rich man, however, had no compassion for Lazarus. He was filled with contempt and disgust toward Lazarus. Lazarus was the stinging eyesore of the manicured neighborhood, the filthy thorn in his pristine flesh—a daily nuisance. Lazarus's putrid stench polluted the air around him. He and his pathetic kind didn't belong in the neighborhood. Why on earth didn't he try to get a job, pull himself up by his own bootstraps, instead of depending on others? If he took better care of himself, he wouldn't be in this position.

Why, oh why did Lazarus gaze at him with his sorrowful eyes full of misery? Why did he dare to look to him every day in hopes of getting something to eat? Didn't he get the point that he was unwanted? Instead of taking the easy way out as a beggar, he should get a hold of himself and let go of his laziness. Where were his parents and family? Why wasn't the synagogue taking care of Lazarus? Maybe the rich man thought about getting the city council to pass some ordinances forbidding panhandlers sitting at the entrance of people's homes, street corners, or at the market.

The rich man didn't have time or energy to be bothered with Lazarus and his situation. He had his own problems and projects, things to do and people to see. He was consumed with making sure he had enough money for retirement so he wouldn't wind up like Lazarus. And anyway, everyone wanted a piece of him, everyone and every cause were tugging on his purse strings, hoping to squeeze some money out of him. And so every day as the rich man came and went from his estate, he stepped over and around Lazarus, pretending not to see Lazarus, until he no longer really saw him or gave him a second thought. He rendered Lazarus invisible. Lazarus faded into background scenery, just another thing on the road.

Old Lazarus finally died. His death is the only thing that freed him from his earthly misery. And Lazarus's death freed the rich man from what was, to him, the inconvenience of Lazarus's life. He was glad to be rid of the nuisance of Lazarus. That piece of trash finally found its rightful place in the dumpster. Quite honestly, Lazarus was better off dead.

Well, our rich man carried on with his life with nary another thought of Lazarus. That is, until *he* died—and woke up from his stupor to a living hell. How interesting that it was in his torment that he happened to look away from himself long enough to really see Lazarus. His Lazarus, the Lazarus that sat at his gate day in and day out, was now sitting in one of the most important places in paradise: right next to Father Abraham. And the rich man, well, he was separated from them both.

I have to wonder if many of us rich ones who profess the name of Jesus will be begging those who were our Lazaruses in this life for a mere drop of cold water to slake our thirst in torment.

BEHOLD, OUR TEACHERS!

Throughout our lives God has placed many teachers, learned ones, we pupils have much to learn from. Lazaruses. Angels—messengers of grace. Agents of salvation, delivering the most essential and important life lessons. Like what really matters and what will last. They teach us how to live. And they teach us we're not as good or as great as we think we are. Humility. Some of them are far better human beings, far better Christians, than we may ever be—full of the fruit of the Spirit while we are mostly full of ourselves. They teach us God has a lot more work to do in us and in our churches and our systems. They teach us that even the best of our churches and systems aren't as holy or as just as we once believed them to be. They are eye-openers. They teach us to see injustices we were blind to.

When it comes to love, sacrifice, and bravery, they show us the ropes. They demonstrate hard work. They teach us that outside forces, circumstances, systems, not laziness or a lack of will, frequently are why many are in their position. They help us understand and see with God's eyes. They show us that we are the ones who are poor and wretched and that we should be sitting at their feet, at their gate, at their cardboard box, detention center, in their nursing home room, or cell, if you will.

Most of the time though, we refuse to see our Lazaruses as God's messengers because they don't suit our notions of a teacher or of angelic beings who are full of grace and wisdom and good tidings for us or anyone else. In fact, we don't consider them worthy of our time, attention, or respect. Maybe not even our money. It comes out in seemingly little things like our attitudes toward people like my brother Marco, whose skin is much darker than mine and who has faced small and great indignities alike. These range from coworkers refusing to call him by his name and instead calling him Pedro in reference to a movie, to being harassed at the northern border on his return from a family trip to Niagara Falls under suspicions of being a terrorist. Our small attitudes and behaviors turn to atrocities when we unsee and dehumanize others instead of welcoming them as gifts. We erase others from our vision.

Why? Because we foolishly believe they cannot do a thing for us. Offering our love and affection to them and courting their love and affection will get us nowhere, or so we think. Truth be told, we

> **Our small attitudes and behaviors turn to atrocities when we unsee and dehumanize others instead of welcoming them as gifts.**

believe we are superior to them. And so we ignore them. Dismiss and devalue them. Treat them with contempt. Bully and abuse them. Leave them for dead on the road to Jericho or in the desert on their trek to the United States or in front of a store in lower Manhattan. We deport them. Herd them onto reservations. Put their children in cages. Erect makeshift concentration camps. Make sure they can't live in our neighborhoods. Unjustly incarcerate them in droves. Fail to visit them in nursing homes. Let them rot in underfunded and undercared for schools. Or in mental hospitals. Or in group homes. Dismiss their point of view and ignore their cries. We shun them. We murder them. We abort them.

We isolate them through unjust laws and behaviors. And we segregate ourselves from them. We find new and improved ways to separate ourselves from them and them from us. Sometimes it's through technicalities in our housing or zoning ordinances or in our school systems. Other times we form caste systems based on ethnicity, wealth, gender, popularity, intelligence, or beauty.

There are many ways to trample on our Lazaruses. Many ways to unsee them. Remember: out of sight, out of mind. And if they are out of sight and thus out of mind, we falsely believe we have no responsibility for them! We hate them while singing our worship songs and convincing ourselves that we are safe from wrongdoing. We fail to realize that we are heretics because of the content of our action or inaction, which reveals the content of our character.

TEACHABLE SPIRITS

First John 4:20-21 tells us: "If anyone boasts, 'I love God,' and goes right on hating his brother or sister, thinking nothing of it, he is a liar. If he won't love the person he can see, how can he love the God he can't see? The command we have from Christ is blunt: Loving God includes loving people. You've got to love both" (*The Message*).

We have our share of experiences, education, answers, and successes—mostly results of privilege but also of self-delusional and self-constructed pedestals we stand on to wax eloquently and from which to look down on people—to justify our action or inaction. The rich man had his reasons and justifications and was pleased enough with them and himself to ignore Lazarus. As Sally Lloyd-Jones insightfully points out in the

Jesus Storybook Bible, we look down on others because we are not looking up at God.

While we may never utter aloud the thoughts our superiority complex speaks, privately we are convinced we have a thing or two to teach these "losers" about life. If they'd just take our advice they'd be better off. But *them* teach *us* anything? Well, no way. They have nothing to offer us. If they did, they wouldn't be in whatever poor condition and situation they find themselves. Obviously, if they were better people, they wouldn't have failed at life. They need what *we* have to offer. Our pity. They are lucky to get our charity. And when we offer it they had better be thankful, not ungrateful wretches!

We are sadly mistaken.

Woefully mistaken.

It is true, not all of us will wake up in hell. However, some of us, like the rich man in the story, will. Still, every one of us will be judged. Only then will we rue the days of self-interest and of our self-aggrandizing efforts. Our greatest wish will be to turn back the clock. In our loathsome states we'll torment ourselves with thoughts like *If only we knew then what we know now!* But by then it'll be too late. And the thing is, we did know and do know better now. We ignore the way of Jesus because it is inconvenient or because we are too busy or because our ultimate allegiance is found elsewhere.

Our self-interest in our own agendas blinds us to others. We power through life thinking that if we get what we want when we want it, then we'll have time for others. Of course, there are seasons when we must pay particular attention and focus on those right in front of us—maybe it's caring for a chronically ill spouse or parent. Or maybe it's being a parent to young children who require most of the energy in our waking moments. And yet these too are our Lazaruses. Our teachers! In those moments, if we peer outside of ourselves and situations, we can see and literally offer a cup of cold water—or a cup of refreshing grace—to those right at our gates.

I worry about us as a church when we ignore and bad mouth the immigrant, undocumented or not, the refugee, the poor, the physically or mentally sick, the elderly, disabled, imprisoned, and other vulnerable and marginalized people, including children. And ignoring doesn't just entail walking past them on the street or failing to give that with which God has entrusted us. Ignoring also entails supporting and voting for bad laws, that is, unjust laws that worsen their plight. I really do worry when we railroad the very people Jesus made a beeline for.

It's one reason Jesus tells us that the eye is the lamp of the body and that if our eyes are unhealthy, our whole body is full of darkness "And," he says, "if the light you think you have is actually darkness, how deep that darkness is!" (Matthew 6:22-23 NLT). It's also why James tells us to be quick to listen and slow to speak (James 1:19).

May God give us teachable spirits!

The only question for us is, will we be pupils? Will we sit at Lazarus's feet or at Lazarus's gate? Will we practice this form of *kenōsis*? Our teachers might be too poor or too ashamed to find themselves around us. Maybe we live in too gated of a community or church—a community or church that keeps Jesus and his messengers out.

THE END OF THE AGE WEDDING FEAST

I trust that as a follower of Jesus I will be at the wedding feast. But I think that with privileged others I will be far away from the VIP seats during the wedding feast of the Lamb. Many of the Lazaruses that we overlooked, disparaged, ignored, devalued—the people that we've done outright violence to by turning away from their suffering and erasing their lives, many of these whose only hope has been in God—will be sitting next to Father Abraham. Closer to Jesus. The rest of us, while there, we'll be in the nosebleed section of the feast, though eternally grateful and full of joy to be present.

7

Rich Toward God

Riches I heed not, nor man's empty praise,
Thou mine Inheritance, now and always:
Thou and Thou only, first in my heart,
High King of Heaven, my Treasure Thou art.

"Be Thou My Vision"

ey! What's up? So good to hear from you!" "Marlena, I have something to tell you. You are one of the only people who won't think we're crazy." In a split second, possibilities zip through my mind, bees in a beehive flying in a thousand directions. I have no idea what she is about to say. "What is it?" I ask, on edge. With bated breath, she lunges forward with her revelation. "We're thinking about giving our house away to a couple we have been mentoring. They could use it."

She waited for me to weigh in, my judgment.

I answered, "It doesn't surprise me in the least bit." I paused a moment. "If anyone would do this, it's you two. How like Jesus of you!" Then I asked what to me seemed like the next logical question. "But where will you live?" At the time they had three children with one on the way. "I don't know. We're praying and looking around."

It's not like my friends are rolling in the dough. Far from it. Almost the opposite. They qualify for Medicaid. They make the most of what they have, stretching their food and resources to the max to feed not only themselves but guests. When I think of them, I think of the widow of Zarephath whose flour was not used up and whose olive oil jug ran over with oil after she gave the prophet Elijah the last of her last (1 Kings 17:7-16).

When we lived a few blocks away from one another, I'd ask, "Do you want me to bring anything?" And she'd reply, "No, just bring yourself." At one point, after I had prayed for a miraculous way to get a new mattress—the coils and springs were taking up residence in our backs—she told me she and her husband were going to gift us with the new mattress. I asked, "Are you kidding?" I tried to dissuade them, tried to tell them all the reasons why they should hang on to the money for themselves, but they would have none of it. Finally, we accepted.

Her husband is one of the hardest workers I know, working full-time and managing to spend as much time as he can with the family. But with her at home and their *very* modest income and a growing family, most days they teeter on the point of not making it. But somehow, they always make do, always add one more guest, delighted to squeeze in another around the table. They have consciously and conscientiously created a lifestyle in which they can be available to others, available to give. They offer the gift of presence and cultivate a culture of generosity as individuals and as a family.

From a human perspective, giving their house away is a no-go. I can imagine more than one financial adviser going berserk, having a cardiac arrest, wondering if they are out of their living minds. This reckless generosity of theirs flows out of their love for Jesus. It flows out of their poverty. They are widows with their widow's mite whose generosity stops Jesus in his tracks. He takes note of their actions, and he records them for posterity's sake. How fortunate am I. I am one of the many beneficiaries of their riches.

No doubt, my friends have encountered the risen Christ. When they break bread with us in their home, our eyes are opened, and Shawn and I realize we've been with Jesus. The light of their lives emanates from their tiny home. Their generosity isn't contingent on having more money. I seldom hear them talk about money or lack of it. They defy the life of scarcity and live out of the abundance of the kingdom. Like the Macedonian churches, "their overflowing joy and their extreme poverty welled up in rich generosity" (2 Corinthians 8:2). More messengers of grace in my life. Interestingly enough, many of the most generous people I know are poor.

> Many of the most generous people I know are poor.

A VOW OF POVERTY?

It reminds me of the countless studies demonstrating that the poor are the most generous and compassionate. In a piece for *Psychology Today*, Utpal Dholakia cites the results from some of these studies: "low social class participants were more generous and believed they should give more of their annual income to charity (4.95 percent vs. 2.95 percent). . . . Contrarily, other research has found that higher social class individuals are more unethical. They are more likely to take things from others, lie, and cheat."

This is why the Roman Catholic Church and many others tell us that we encounter Christ in the poor. Does all this mean poverty in itself is virtuous? By no means. There are poor charlatans and rich charlatans. But poverty and poverty of spirit frequently go hand in hand.

Wealth can build walls between us and God and us and others. In Matthew 13:22 Jesus tells us, "the worries of this life and the deceitfulness of wealth choke the word, making it unfruitful." Should we each take a vow of poverty then? Divest ourselves of the riches that keep us from entering the kingdom of heaven or that make it exceedingly hard to do so?

Yes.

We are to count ourselves dead to our possessions, poor when it comes to our possessions tangible and intangible. In following Jesus, we give it all up to "possess God," as Bishop Clement of Alexandria said. On any reading of God's Word, the early church fathers and mothers and anyone else who takes Jesus seriously, we find neither our money nor the riches of our lives belong to us. All of it belongs to God and to our neighbor. Our money and our lives are to be conduits of grace for the love of Christ and the world.

> **Our money and our lives are to be conduits of grace for the love of Christ and the world.**

God so loved the world that he *gave*. Those of us who profess to adore God will offer up ourselves and everything we are and have to him and for the life of the world. It is basic Christianity—self-giving, *kenōsis*, a life of generosity. "You know the grace of our Lord Jesus Christ," Paul tells us, "that though he was rich, yet for your sake he became poor, so that you through his poverty might become rich" (2 Corinthians 8:9).

Our money and our lives are not ours to withhold from others. Our incomes, our homes, our cars, our clothes, our shoes, our coats, our food, even the direction of our lives are not our own. If we encounter someone in need and have the means, then we give. What we have belongs to them as Saint Basil so wisely and unabashedly points out, "The bread in your cupboard belongs to the hungry man; the coat hanging unused in your closet belongs to the man who needs it; the shoes rotting in your closet belong to the man who has no shoes; the money which you put in the bank belongs to the poor."

Acquiring even a smidge of the generosity of God will require more of us becoming even more generous with our time and resources. Generous in spending our time in dismantling systems that induce poverty. God isn't content to let us take up residence in our stinginess or isolation. It is possible to become like my friends—at the ready to hand over our homes in an instant. Such behavior is not even remotely new. It is the way of Jesus and has been happening for centuries. It is basic Christianity. We are to use our gifts generously.

Members of the early church were especially renowned among unbelievers for their generosity, for risking their lives to care for the sick and bury the dead when a plague spread across North Africa and Western Europe in 250 AD. It was everyday ordinary folk doing works of mercy and demonstrating generosity and compassion to those who could never repay them.

They did so with the full knowledge that as they were nursing the sick and burying the dead, they were putting their own lives at risk. These believers were different from their pagan counterparts who left people, including the elderly and babies, to die. The unbelievers, understandably, were worried about catching the plague. Christians were too, but they counted love and obedience to Christ as greater than their lives. Thus, they could live generously in caring for other Christians *as wells as those who didn't believe.*

We are told that Bishop Cyprian of Carthage, "enjoined the city's Christians to give aid to their persecutors and to care for the sick. He urged the rich to donate funds and the poor to volunteer their service for relief efforts, making no distinction between believers and pagans." They functioned as the first hospitals, nurses, hospices, and funeral homes—a tradition continuing to this day.

WEALTH AND MODESTY

At every turn God confronts our greed and our tendency to hoard our goods, our money, and our gifts. Does it mean we live like Jesus, as paupers with nowhere to lay our heads, owning nothing?

For some people it will.

For others it won't.

But one thing we can all do is confess our love of money. You know people in Alcoholics Anonymous confess their addictions. What if we had an AA confession in our churches? "Hi, I am _____ and I love money." Then we could follow up with, "This is how it has led to all sorts of evil." We could then ask for prayer and a laying on of hands and accountability. Some pastors will be first in line. I am not talking about the faithful, bivocational, poverty-stricken pastors in our churches who deserve more pay and more rest. These are the pastors we should bow before in honor of their selfless work and sacrifice.

I speak of those who live on par with millionaires who are hoarding instead of giving. I speak of those who think that godliness and church work are a means to financial gain (1 Timothy 6:5). Those who shake down the poor and the widow and other folks who give in good faith. Yet in reality their tithes pave the way for these money-loving leaders to live like kings and queens in palatial living quarters, to eat the most exquisite foods, to participate in a globe-trotting lifestyle—to live in "unapologetic opulence." If this were the 1980s, they'd be featured on the television show *Lifestyles of the Rich and Famous* with Robin Leach.

These leaders of ours *should* be the first in line to confess. And the rest of us should follow suit. But let's not hold our breath waiting for them. We'll turn blue in the face and die before any sort of confession takes place. Instead, let us lead the leaders and hold them accountable.

Still, there are those like Pope Francis who choose to live in a simple residence, in a guest house, rather than in a luxurious residence.

It is very possible we will go into poverty, some form of poverty—hear me—for the sake of others. Obedient generosity will require sacrifice. As a result of our obedient generosity we won't always get our way or always have what we want. The more we practice, the more accustomed we'll become. In doing so we make room for joy.

I have a warm, royal blue, Columbia jacket that I bought at Dick's Sporting Goods on sale for twenty dollars. If I encounter someone who needs a coat this winter, man, woman, or child, and it fits them, it belongs to them. I can easily get another one.

Maybe we can hang onto some of our shoes and coats and clothes and ask God to bring someone across our path who needs them. Store them in our closet until that person in need is in front of us. As the *Didache* instructs us, "Let thine alms sweat into thine hands until thou knowest to whom thou art giving."

What about our churches? So much space goes unused during weekdays. And in the cold weather. Could we house the homeless in our churches on cold nights? Some churches do this. "They stink, have lice, bed bugs," I've heard said. Some might. (Though I worked at a private Christian university where students of all social classes had bed bugs so we know bed bugs do not show a preference for the poor.) But could we not find creative ways to shelter them? Community agencies deal with this all of the time, they have wisdom for us. Could we work together to be the arms of Christ embracing those who need it most in the shelter of our sanctuaries? Do we think twice about those who have no place to stay while we enjoy the warmth and shelter of our homes?

Maybe instead of building bigger buildings we can build affordable housing on our church property or homeless shelters with individual rooms so the homeless and the cold feel safe. We could share our time shares and vacation homes and extras of whatever we have. We could take less in our bonus and offer more people jobs. We could offer a piece of bread, a drink of water. We can allow others to enjoy what we have too. What if we sent the poor on vacation?

PULLING A JUDAS?

We're not gonna pull a Judas and mutter under our breaths in judgment that Mary should've thought twice before smashing

98

her expensive perfume bottle to anoint Jesus' feet. That instead she should've sold it and given the proceeds to the poor. There are times of celebration, times to smash our perfume bottles for God and others.

We are to hold it all loosely. We are to be marked by generosity toward God and toward one another. Paul gives us a rule of life when it comes to money and generosity: "Command those who are rich in this present world not to be arrogant nor to put their hope in wealth, which is so uncertain, but to put their hope in God, *who richly provides us with everything for our enjoyment*" (1 Timothy 6:17 emphasis added).

We are to enjoy. God gave Adam and Eve the Garden and animals and food and each other for mutual enjoyment. God is not harsh, stingy, or tight-fisted. There is a time for everything, including feasting and celebration. God himself called for celebrations. Flip through Scripture and see. "Go and enjoy choice food and sweet drinks, and send some to those who have nothing prepared. This day is holy to our Lord. Do not grieve, for the joy of the LORD is your strength," Nehemiah told the people after Ezra the Priest and the Levites read aloud God's word (Nehemiah 8:10). Heaven and kingdom come are talked about as a feast. We are to enjoy God and life and one another *and* live generously. No tension there. It's a way of life. Some people never enjoy anything out of guilt. That's unhealthy. Has not God given us everything for our enjoyment?

Paul goes on to explain, "Command them to do good, to be rich in good deeds, and to be generous and willing to share" (1 Timothy 6:18). And finally, "In this way they will lay up treasure for themselves as a firm foundation for the coming age, so that they may take hold of the life that is truly life" (v. 19). What is the line between conspicuous consumption and simple enjoyment? Sometimes it is obvious and other times it is not. When it isn't, it will call for individual discernment in concert with the communal discernment and wisdom to know exactly what to do with our time and money.

We know this: those of us who are rich are to live modestly, to lay up treasures in a coming age by giving to God by giving to others. We are to be rich toward God. If modesty is "freedom from vanity and conceit," with synonymous or related words being *reserve*, *decency*, *humble*, and *polite*, what would that look like in relation to our wealth and our current situation? What would it mean to live with reserve, in an unassuming way, that we might pour ourselves out on behalf of others?

It might look like doing all we can to support Jesus. Remember, Jesus and his disciples had generous benefactors, those who supported them with their presence, service, and finances so Jesus and the Twelve could minister unencumbered about concern for their daily bread. So they could have a day off. A lot of benefactors were women. Luke 8:1-3 says,

> Jesus traveled about from one town and village to another, proclaiming the good news of the kingdom of God. The Twelve were with him, and also some women who had been cured of evil spirits and diseases: Mary (called Magdalene) from whom seven demons had come out; Joanna the wife of Chuza, the manager of Herod's household; Susanna; and many others. These women were helping to support them out of their own means.

AM I MY BROTHER AND SISTER'S KEEPER?

Those who minister are free to minister because of the generosity of their supporters. When Jesus teaches his disciples, and us, to pray for our daily bread, he expects we'll be the daily bread for others. That we will gladly tear off a piece of our bread and hand it to our brothers and sisters and children. He has been known to multiply a modest little lunch of five loaves and two fish. He multiplies our daily little loaves *after* we rip off a piece in communion with others. *Not before.* Whether we are wealthy in relationships, talent, time, earthly possessions, energy, or all of them, we too are to be Jesus' benefactors, daily bread for God and others, by giving what is already his to him, ministry, the poor, and each other.

John Wesley was one of the richest men in England because of the number of tracts he sold. His tracts were pamphlets of information explaining the Christian life. But instead of living on his income, he practically lived on the amount he made when he started out. When Wesley died, he had nothing on earth save what was in his pockets. He had given it all away almost as soon as he made it: "Wesley preached that Christians should not merely tithe, but give away all extra income once the family and creditors were taken care of. He believed that with increasing income, the Christian's standard of giving should increase, not his standard of living."

I remember hearing of another within my lifetime who did this: the late Rich Mullins. He lived on what the average working-class American made and gave the rest away. It is a rare thing, but not as rare as we might think. Pope Francis is a model of generosity. And yet it's not just these well-known men. Women too are examples to us. Macrina the Younger, older sister to Basil the Great (who I quoted earlier) and Gregory of Nyssa, two church fathers, divested herself of her inherited wealth on behalf of the poor. Where do you think Basil the Great acquired his attitude toward money and the poor? No doubt his sister, Macrina. Gregory of Nyssa tells us himself that he and his brother Basil learned everything from her.

Recently I learned of middle school students living in inner-city St. Louis, Missouri, who give generously of the little they have for others. There is a lack of socioeconomic diversity because those who can, leave. They all have the same exact school uniform: a polo shirt and khaki pants. The only deviation is their shoes and the hoodies each student chooses to wear every day of the year no matter the temperature. Their teacher Isaac told me he could recognize each student based on their hoodie and shoes until Christmas time. And it is in their generosity with what they wear and have that we can learn. Isaac describes it for us. Read carefully:

> After Christmas break, something interesting happened, the students began to swap hoodies. Students would forego wearing their hoodie for a day because one of their friends who didn't have a nice hoodie wanted to "drip" for a day. (Drip is their slang for dapper, fresh, clean, cool, etc.) By the end of the year, the hoodie swap became a staple of our school community.
>
> At the end of the day, students scramble around the whole school because they have to get their hoodie, headphones, and cellphones back from other students in the building before their buses arrive. Students will give their phones to their peers who are having a bad day and

want to listen to music. Their phone will be out of sight for hours at a time because of the sharing economy at Fanning Middle. The interesting thing is, the sharing economy is NOT supported by teachers, it is entirely student driven. Most teachers find it frustrating when students run out of class at the end of the day to retrieve or return a personal item. Parents worry that students will lose their items when given to their friends. I've witnessed several parents become verbally hostile after seeing their students allow their friends to wear the clothes they recently purchased for their child. In the midst of adult hostility, the students share much—or more than ever.

Most of my students go hungry at least once a week. Although I assume this would mean they are more stingy with their food, that assumption couldn't be more false. To the chagrin of many teachers, me included, students routinely pull out snacks in class. The reason this process is annoying, is because the students will proceed to share their snack with each and every student that asks until the snack is gone. I once rewarded a student who formerly struggled academically with a bag of chips for receiving an A on a summative assessment. That student proceeded to give away each and every one of his chips to other students in the class. They share food, drinks, and anything else they have regardless of their personal desires.

Maybe all we have is one potato chip to share in Jesus' name. Maybe it is a hoodie or a phone. How might we allow another to "drip" for the day? There are women and children, students at Fanning Middle School, and thousands of saints who are exhibiting the generosity of Jesus this moment all over the world. No one knows who they are. But many of their names are written in the Book of Life. Jesus takes note of them. He looks at them in delight, cheers raucously for them from the stands of life because they are living as he lived. We should too.

May Jesus' grace be made manifest in and through our lives. For though he was rich, for our sakes he became poor that through his poverty we might become rich (2 Corinthians 8:9).

Amen.

8

Memento Mori

*Teach us to number our days, that we may
apply our hearts unto wisdom.*

PSALM 90:12 KJV

*Each man's death diminishes me, for I am
involved in mankind. Therefore, send not to know
for whom the bell tolls, it tolls for thee.*

JOHN DONNE

The thought of death haunts me.

Impending death.

In his Rule, Saint Benedict says "to have the expectation of death daily before one's eyes." That practice is also known as *memento mori*. It's no problem for me. Even at twenty-five years old, I thought to myself, *I am a quarter of a century old. I could die any time.* Most every day I think to myself, *I'm gonna die.*

Don't ask me why.

I am not sure.

But here's a guess. It could be my natural sensitivity and proclivities. Even my oldest daughter, Iliana, cried and cried—actually, she wailed—when she was three years old at the sight of three wilted roses. They were the roses we bought for her third birthday, one for each year. That wailing at the reality of death, that was natural for her. The floodgates opened; it took us a long time to soothe her and calm her down after she witnessed the end to life and beauty and what the roses stood for—our love. Wilted roses: a stark picture of death for our three-year-old.

Or maybe the daily thought of death is the identifying mark left by the branding iron of childhood poverty. Or seeing family members like one of the loves of my life, my abuelita, on her death bed three days before she turned eighty-nine. Abuelita was strong, beautiful, always looked made up when she went out, dyed her hair dark brown until the very end, was a hard worker, and overflowed with contagious laughter. We were the best of friends. Her name: Juanita Fidelia Deida Ramos Negron. I remember one summer night home from college: I was twenty-one and she eighty-eight. We cackled late into the night. Couldn't catch our breaths because we were laughing so hard. Side-splitting laughter and wiping our tears. We were probably laughing at someone else's expense. Probably at Mami's. And it was probably over one of Mami's endearing idiosyncrasies. I am sure it was.

Occasionally, I have dreams where Abuelita and I are talking and giggling, and then I remember. Death barges into my dream, unannounced and unwelcomed. It reminds me Abuelita is dead. My utter joy because of her presence comes to an abrupt halt. Then I say in Spanish (while hoping it's not true),

"But Abuelita, you are dead!" And just like that, no matter how furiously I grasp after her, the dream ends. She slides through my fingers, floats away: a shade, a puff of smoke, a vanishing dream. Just a second before, she was incarnate. Sorrow comes flooding in again.

How I long to embrace Abuelita and inhale the familiar smell of her skin! How I love her! I think of Abuelita nearly every day of my life—wonder what she is doing in paradise. I carry her within my cells. She is lodged in my memory. I have her wooden rosary beads prominently displayed in my home. The beads are one of the few of her possessions left. If you look at me, you might glimpse Abuelita in my face, except I am slightly paler. My mom and dad say I am shaped like her. Her life remains in me, in my three daughters too, though they will never know her. Not in this life. Only the beads. They only know of the rosary beads.

I can't talk about Abuelita without mentioning Abuelito. Abuelito died not long after they moved to West Palm Beach, Florida. They decided to move in with Uncle Lenny (Leonardo) and his family for a while. To share their time with him and his wife, Elizabeth, and the other grandkids, my cousins, and to get away from the snow.

I never got to go to Abuelito's funeral.

My parents couldn't afford to take us.

All I know is that Abuelito's remnants remain stashed away in a West Palm Beach mausoleum. For the life of them my parents cannot remember the burial site's name, nor have they traveled there since. The internet doesn't render me much help either. Just his date of birth and date of his death.

Juan F. Deida.

F stands for Francisco.

I can round out his person just a little. Some facts about Abuelito: he was an orphan. Then adopted. He drove yellow taxi cabs in New York City and occasionally picked up celebrities. It gave my abuelito, abuelita, mami, and Uncle Lenny something to talk about around the dinner table. The Deida Ramos-Negron family lived in Spanish Harlem near Columbia University for a good chunk of time before they moved back to Puerto Rico. In Spanish Harlem the Mafia owned their apartment building but treated them well and with respect. Like royalty. At one point Abuelito and Abuelita were entrepreneurs—business people. They had a food truck in the 1950s. And a small, what amounts to a convenience store in their garage in the 1970s and 1980s. If they were young and alive now, they'd probably be well off. But Abuelito died of a heart attack on December 26, 1990. I was twelve. Uncle Lenny died a year later. After Abuelito and Uncle Lenny died, Abuelita moved back in with us.

To the undiscerning eye, his name, the date of his birth, and the date of his death are what's left of his existence. Unless you count the words I write presently. That's why a twinge of sadness lingers in me. Abuelito brimmed with life and laughter. In fact, he elicited belly laughter from my entire family on a near constant basis. He being shaped like a squat Latin Buddha and what with his daily pretending to strum his stomach as if it were a guitar, only added to our hysterics. There was heft to his existence. He was a simple man. A hard-working man. Akin to a modern-day Uber or Lyft driver with whom you'd have a cheerful and interesting conversation and leave better for it. A co-owner of a food truck, with Abuelita, which people flocked to. A name and two dates on either side of a dash hardly do him justice.

My ancestors, even those far removed from my consciousness, those I've never known or have known to exist, live and speak through me—in my genetics, in my body. In my gait. I wonder about my genealogy on my mom's and dad's sides, about the unnamed and unfaced and unrecorded who have contributed to who I am right now. Taino Indians. Caribbean Indians. Africans. Spaniards. The Scottish coming on my dad's side through his parents. Am I like some of them? I suppose so. But I won't know the details anytime soon. Maybe in the age to come it will all be revealed. Maybe in paradise a whole host of relatives will be there to greet me—relatives I've never known.

I am tied to more than my own past. I am tied to many pasts—the pasts of those who came before me all the way back to our ancient parents: Adam and Eve. Did Jesus pore over his own genealogy? What a motley crew and treasure trove of ancestors he had! Jesus carried his ancestral genes in himself. The earthiness of it all. I wonder if Mary and Joseph recounted the stories of their ancestors. Who did Jesus resemble?

SKULLS, SMILING SKELETONS, DANCING SKELETONS

Indeed, remembrance of death, or memento mori, is a long-standing Christian practice. Some of the ancients opted for keeping skulls on their desks to remind them of their own mortality. Others had coffins in their studies. Sister Theresa Aletheia Noble, a Roman Catholic nun, points out a few of the ways in which our ancestors in the faith remembered their death: "Saint Francis of Assisi once signed a blessing to Brother Leo with the tau cross and a small drawing of a skull. Pope Alexander VII commissioned Italian artist Bernini to make a coffin that he kept in his bedroom along with a marble skull for his desk to remind him of the brevity of life."

During the late medieval period, upon crossing the threshold of a church, one might happen upon a mural depicting the *Danse Macabre* or the "Dance of Death." In these murals we'd see skeletons and smorgasbord of human beings: rich, poor, men, women, children, and the disabled, all dancing with skeletons. Was this merely a grisly obsession with death and skeletal corpses on the part of artists and churches and laypeople and saints?

It was not.

Even in an age of wars, plagues, high infant mortality rates, and premodern medicine, an age where people were much more familiar with death and died younger—it was possible to live an "eat, drink, and be merry" sort of life without giving much thought to the reality of "because tomorrow you will die." Skulls on desks or necklaces and skeletons dancing on church walls were stark reminders of impending death. They were not fashion brands à la 1980s death metal bands or assorted biker groups.

Old age, aching bones, sickness, debilitation, and more and more friends dying can also serve as memento mori. A few years ago, I was the minister of pastoral care at my previous church. Basically, the associate pastor. As a result, among other things, I've visited people at their bedsides in their own homes, nursing homes, hospitals, and hospice care. Parishioners even joked that "Death must be knocking on their door" and that they must be in really "terrible condition" if they were at the top of my visitation list. And that sentiment wasn't without reason; so many were ill in our congregation that those in the worst condition were visited first by me. I had trained other pastorally inclined men and women in the grace of visitation, and I delegated to them the pastoral care visits of those who were less sick.

While there, I conducted so many funerals I've lost count. Not all the deceased had attended our church. Some just considered us their church. Other times, the funeral homes called and asked me to conduct a funeral for those who had no church or pastor. I did my level best to treat each funeral homily as a work of art, to pay tribute, however little I could, to a life. However, funerals for particular people were especially challenging because of how badly they lived and how badly they treated those around them.

And yet, how does one measure the value of human life?

Being among the sick and dying taught me that life is indeed precious. And that people in difficult circumstances whose bodies or minds or both are betraying them can live well. After being among so many sick and dying people, I can declare with confidence that God's measurement of the value of human life and our own are as far as the east is from the west. Life is truly precious. We, on the other hand, are habituated to render too many lives and life itself nearly worthless. We live in an overwhelmingly nihilistic time even though many of us in richer countries have nearly all of our needs and many of our wants met. We have everything but act like we have nothing, like the older son in the parable of the prodigal and like Adam and Eve.

We devalue and take much for granted in the way we treat people, speak to them, and dehumanize them in our hearts; or the way we treat creation; or how we hide the poor, immigrant, refugee, disabled, elderly, sick, dying from our view; or how we shoot the wounded within the church; or the various theologies and social and economic policies we forge are any indication.

Some of us might need skulls, dancing skeletons, smiling skeletons, and *Danse Macabre* murals to remind us of the brevity of life. Or perhaps remembrance of our deaths will come by actually visiting the sick and the dying, as Jesus would have us do, instead of forgetting them because they are out of sight and out of mind. Of course, we don't objectify or use people just so we can remember our deaths. We visit because we love. But living the life Jesus commands us, and actually doing what he says, means remembrance of death will be part of the normal rhythm of our lives, as it should be. But living means that death will also come to us unexpectedly and uninvited. It interrupts. This we cannot control.

FAST AND SWIFTLY APPROACHING: ONE WEEK

As I write, we are eight days into Lent. But in the last six days I've had three stark reminders of death. Two deaths and a near death. Uninvited memento mori, not in a dream but in life. First, a forty-one-year-old high school classmate of my husband's, Matt, died six days ago in a tragic car accident. His thirteen-year-old daughter, who was traveling with him, is injured but survived. She was riding along with her daddy, maybe not a care in the world, and then in a split second he was no more on this earth. When Shawn told me about it, I immediately had a knot in my stomach. While Matt's death was fresh on our minds, three days later Shawn's larger-than-life Uncle Larry, as strong and jolly and as short of a man one would ever meet, who had a twinkle in his blue eyes and a continual smile, succumbed to prostate cancer that metastasized. His funeral is in a few days. And his absence? Palpable.

And today, day six: Shawn was T-boned after picking up our youngest, four-year-old Isabella. Air bags deployed. Upon finding out, I immediately left work and got to them before the ambulance even though I had to drive fifteen minutes to get there. I feared what I would find. After the impact, Shawn heard Isabella's piercing cries. He feared turning around to find a pool of blood and fatal injuries—all on his watch.

Soon after I arrived, relief. I sent Shawn off in the ambulance with Isabella. He seemed all right as did she. Our van, not so much. I couldn't get into the ambulance because I had to figure out what to do about our two oldest daughters. I couldn't be both at the hospital and pick them up from school. Since it all happened so close to their schools and halfway through the school day, I figured I should be the one to pick them up, tell them what happened, and then head to the ER. We finally arrived at the hospital only to find Shawn and Isabella ready to leave. No tests were run, only a dose of Motrin given. Isabella has only a black eye and a tiny cut on her face. No internal injuries. Shawn is scheduled to see his primary physician early in the morning. The other driver refused medical treatment and drove away. Today could've been extremely tragic. But it turned out to be the kind of traumatizing event that makes one sick to their stomach and simultaneously grateful for life.

However, in the blink of an eye Matt lost his life six days ago. His family is bereft. Left behind. Full of fresh throbbing pain. Internal injuries to their whole being. Wrecked. His wife and children are unable to breathe the sigh of relief I did when I found out Isabella's injuries were minor and Shawn was virtually fine. A wife is now without her loving husband and best friend. Three young children are without their father. Uncle Larry's wife, Janet, and children and grandchildren are grief stricken. We are sad to not have him here. But my two oldest daughters, Iliana and Valentina, and I still have Daddy and Isabella. Today we are not bereft. But tomorrow we could be. Inexplicable.

Memento mori.

DAYS OF OUR LIVES: LIVING IN *KAIROS* TIME

Those of us who come by memento mori honestly and easily could be at risk of living paralyzed lives. Fear based on the reality of death is the root of many phobias. Traveling by plane, train, or automobiles, walking on a sidewalk, or riding a bike is risking an accident. Thunderstorms could turn into tornadoes. The most innocent gusts of wind on a sunny day could at once be refreshing and also deadly if they send tree branches crashing down on us. Tripping over our own feet in our homes or outside could lead to fatal head injuries. We live with the possibility of purchasing fruits and vegetables that are contaminated with deadly bacteria. Entering the doctor's office or the hospital in search of healing could leave us infected with a deadly strain of pneumonia or the flu. Choosing to be in a relationship could end in pain. The relationship could go south. Or disease and death could steal our partner away.

Trying to ensure that every decision we make is risk and disappointment free, trying to control our lives and the lives of others in order to eliminate uncertainty isn't living at all. It is comatose living. A form of death. Living is risky business. I don't like that much at all, but the longer I live, the more I comprehend just how fragile and vulnerable we are. The moment we are born, we begin to die.

Life is a great gift and a terrible thing to waste.

As children, when we first learn of death, it is a faint rumor, unreality. We don't pay much attention to it. Unless we are sensitive to such things. Death is like a land far, far away, until it shows up uninvited on our doorstep. Only then do we believe it is real, albeit shrouded in mystery. Most all of us will take our turn in death unless we are the ones living at the very end of the known world, the very last of the living, when Jesus returns in all his glory to finish what he is doing now: making all things new.

> Life is a great gift and a terrible thing to waste.

In light of how death can come to us fast and furious, without notice, what might a healthy posture be? Some of us may very well choose to place a skull or a painting of a skull in a prominent place as a daily reminder that life is fleeting and is much more robust than the tyranny of the urgent. Maybe bust out the skull necklaces and crossbones. Get one painted on the back of our jean jackets and make sure to look at it every day.

We could take lingering walks in the cemetery, pondering the final resting place—the birth and deceased dates etched into the tombstones of those once alive. We might imagine their vitality, their hopes and dreams. And then remember that we too will one day lie in repose, our bodies still in death, and that others may stop to imagine our lives.

Whatever rhythms or icons we choose to use for our practice of memento mori, the hope is that these will catapult us into living a flesh and blood life with our priorities straight. Living a flesh-and-blood life with right-side-up priorities is living in *kairos* time, God's time. About the concept of *kairos*, writer and editor McKinley Valentine says, "In Christian theology, *kairos* is referred to extensively. It has a sense of 'ripeness.' It can be a small moment in one person's life that is ripe, and full, and perfect." Memento mori-ing—if I may use that term—is living and seeing through the brevity-of-life lens. A memento mori posture allows us to more constantly glimpse the "ripe," "full," and "perfect" moments—to live steeped in *kairos* time, to live God's priorities rightly. We remember we are human, instead of superhuman. We live within the bounds of our limits even within breakneck-speed cultures. We don't take life for granted. Little moments produce great joy in the midst of our sufferings and difficulties. Paradoxically, remembering our deaths allows for much more joy in the little things. *Joie de vivre.*

MEANING AND PATH-MAKING

Like all others currently walking on the earth, and all others before us, we need to heed the deep wisdom of Sabbath-keeping because burning the candle at both ends is bad for our health, for our families and friends, for our relationship with God, and even for strangers. Bad for the earth. When we ignore the limits of our humanity and our need for rest, we are Sisy-phuses rolling our stone uphill only in the end to have it roll down back on us. We are Icarus flying to heaven with our wax wings, attempting to transcend our humanity, only to have the sun melt our wings, hurling us to the earth and to our demise.

It is a way of catcalling death. Inhumane. We're wanna be superhumans daily making little and big efforts to transcend the limits of our humanity. And then we wonder why we are so miserable, why we miss the ripe and full moments of our days. The delight and wonder about us. It is arrogant living. Foolish too. Even if it is done and disguised with an air of modesty. Or called "ministry."

But what about making a difference or saving the world? Having an influence? Leaving a legacy? Is that allowed? If we don't push ourselves, we'll never get anything done. Shouldn't we grab life by the horns with the time we do have? Be a mover and a shaker with the little time allotted to us? If we don't, we'll perish in anonymity. We'll die without having been known and admired. Die without having achieved fame.

Yet climbing the ladder of success at the expense of God's kingdom, others, and self poses a mortal danger. The climb may very well yield temporary gains. But why destroy everything and everyone with a rules-don't-apply-to-me sort of attitude? Why put ourselves and others at risk for short-lived pleasures or achievements? Run ourselves and everyone about us into the ground? Is it because we think ourselves above the rules? Or that the wisdom of the ages doesn't apply to us? Or that we won't lose our souls? It takes self-reflection to come to the truth about what is going on inside of us.

BE SOMEBODY!

I cannot get away from Jesus' temptation in the desert. I simply cannot. I think about it all of the time. Picture it happening to me because it does happen to me. Henri Nouwen talks about it too. I'll use my own rendition of the temptation, which is influenced by Nouwen's thoughts: "Jump from the temple and do something spectacular so people will know who you are and like you," Satan whisper-hissed to Jesus while standing on the pinnacle of the temple (Matthew 4). "Or else, you'll be a nobody in this life." This thought can capture us and leave us wild-eyed and in despair. Culture and the media fuel this temptation. It is the water in which we swim. But practicing memento mori can empty our souls of these falsehoods, these devils disguised as angels of light, stave off nihilism, give us a God's eye view—and fill us with God's Spirit and character and joy and priorities. *Kenōsis.*

Practicing memento mori turns our eyes off of these anti-Christs and onto Christ. Practicing memento mori trains us to take off our shoes on the holy ground of the daily *kairos* moments. We slow down enough to notice them. And discover that our lives are full of them. Joy.

At some point in his humanity, Jesus figured out that he was going to die for us. That knowledge conjoined with the Father's will set the priorities of his life. Memento mori limited and constrained him. He didn't travel about the world preaching to all or healing everyone. He could only do so much on a given day and in his one, short life. He had to choose carefully. And so do we. He had to trust his Father, through the work of the Spirit, for the rest. So do we. This trust in his Father for the life his Father had given him allowed Jesus to Sabbath in peace. So can we. It wasn't all up to Jesus—the Father and the Spirit worked with him to accomplish what needed to be done. And it's not all up to us. We have God's help and the church's help.

We are each a part of the body with particular roles in our time (see Romans 12). The limitations and constraints that memento mori reminds us of can be lifesaving. Meaning and path-making in the *kairos* time God has given us will come within our limits and constraints, our boundaries (see Acts 17:26-28). God's life and energy will course through our particular human limits and boundaries. Our human limits and boundaries will serve to channel Christ's life within us into the world, into space and time. God works within our human limits and boundary lines. Of that, we can be sure. Joy.

May God teach us to number our days that our paths may turn from crooked to straight, to wisdom. Let us number our days, practice memento mori, that we might empty ourselves of the foolish notions lodged in our insides. Numbering our days helps us turn aside from the sirens calling out to us in this Vanity Fair-like life and toward Christ—the Alpha and Omega—our all in all—the wisdom of the ages. No doubt Vanity Fair has made its way into the church, and we need to turn away from that too and run to Christ. Lord knows I do!

> God works within our human limits and boundary lines. Of that, we can be sure. Joy.

The philosopher-king Solomon came to a similar conclusion. He tried everything under the sun, everything his soul desired. He followed his heart, made some very stupid decisions, combed the earth in every direction for its wisdom, and yet in the end he found it all meaningless.

His conclusion?

Now all has been heard;
here is the conclusion of the matter:
Fear God and keep his commandments,
for this is the duty of all mankind.

For God will bring every deed into judgment,
including every hidden thing,
whether it is good or evil. (Ecclesiastes 12:13-14)

Memento mori.
Amen.

9

Cradled in the Heart of God

GRATITUDE AND CONTENTMENT

*We never know how strongly we cling to objects until
they are taken away, and he who thinks that he is
attached to nothing, is frequently grandly mistaken, being
bound to a thousand things, unknown to himself.*

JEANNE MARIE BOUVIER DE LA MOTTE GUYON

*Do everything without grumbling or arguing, so that
you may become blameless and pure, "children of God
without fault in a warped and crooked generation." Then
you will shine among them like stars in the sky.*

PHILIPPIANS 2:14-15

We opted to buy our Buick LeSabre based on my brother Kenny's recommendation. He said they were good cars. But really, I liked the look of a black Toyota Avalon much more. We bought our 2005 black LeSabre in 2008, when our oldest, Iliana, was a year old, because it was $4,000 cheaper than the Avalon. At last check, our old faithful LeSabre has 252,652 miles on it. Iliana is twelve.

Unfortunately, the speedometer no longer works, and we are to the point where we don't want to spend the money to have it fixed. I don't know about Shawn, but when I drive it, I monitor my speed by staying behind other cars who are *not* in the passing lane. Should I get pulled over, I can honestly say, "Officer, I have no idea how fast I was driving." If a police officer, or anyone else for that matter, were to pry a little further, they would discover that our fuel gauge doesn't work either. (Actually, pretty much nothing on the instrument panel works—speedometer, fuel gauge, tachometer, temperature gauge.) On a positive note, at least the yellow warning light indicating our car is on empty still works. When it flashes and the bell dings, dings, dings, we know we'd better get gas quickly or we'll be walking and phoning our friends or pastors to give us a ride home.

I have to add another thing to my list: the car's air conditioner met its demise some time ago. Having air conditioning in our vehicles spoiled us to the point that driving in the sweltering summer heat without AC is a trial. Would you believe the gray ceiling fabric sags now too? Of course, you would. I imagine it's because we have the windows open when it's hot out. The hot winds blow through our vehicle and the ceiling fabric comes unglued. As a result, onlookers see what looks like a curtain sagging, hanging on top of the girls' heads in the back seat. We addressed this situation with Christmas ornament colors: red, yellow, green, and blue push pins now keep the fabric from falling onto our heads and from obstructing our view. If you are keeping tally with me, we have the following not working for us: the instrument panel on the dashboard, the air conditioner, and sagging ceiling fabric. And at this point in time, almost everything except the body of the car has been replaced.

Here's the clincher. A couple of weeks ago our mechanic told us we need rear air shocks and coil springs. They are rotten. Rusted. The estimated cost is between $1,500 and $2,000, definitely more than the car is worth. "Since you and Shawn take such good care of your car and the engine is in great condition, you could buy yourself a couple of years if you get it fixed," our mechanic told us. There's one caveat: that's true only if nothing else goes wrong. The plus of fixing it is that we wouldn't have a car payment. That is our goal—not to have another car payment. But what if something else does go wrong? It's all one big gamble. And frankly, sentimentality plays a role here too: I'd hate to see the car go to the junkyard. But it's inevitable.

Then again, I could seriously see myself using duct tape to fix her up if it meant not having a car payment. People do what they need to do to survive. Some use duct tape or leave their car broken as it is because they can't afford to get it fixed or for their insurance premiums to go up if they have insurance at all. And maybe they don't have family members who can lend them the money to fix it or the ability to put it on a credit card. Driving in an obviously battered and bruised car is not one's first choice. Frequently, when we see someone driving a ramshackle car, I'm careful to remind my girls: "If they could afford to fix it, they would. Not everyone has money to fix their cars." Heck, we don't always have money to fix our car: witness the push pins in the ceiling, no air-conditioner, no working instrument panel. Maybe onlookers wonder why we're driving our car.

After Shawn and Isabella were in the car accident and our van was totaled, our insurance paid for a rental vehicle. We were left with our Buick LeSabre and a 2019 Ford Expedition as a rental. We called the Expedition "the tank." It was huge with all sorts of technical bells and whistles.

A rear camera!

A ding-ding-ding if vehicles approached as we backed up!

Little yellow lights flashing on the side mirrors informing us of vehicles on either side!

A sun roof!

Cruise control that would automatically slow down if the vehicle detected another vehicle close ahead!

Heated driver's- and passenger's-side seats!

A trunk that closed automatically at the press of a button!

Oh, and we had doors that automatically locked and opened. We haven't had those in forever.

In the Expedition we sat much higher up than most people. How easy it was to look down on other drivers from on high. Riding in the Expedition reminded me of how tempting it is to judge oneself or others based on the vehicles we drive. I kept thinking to myself, *What a con! If you don't know us you might imagine we're something financially that we aren't. But it's just a rental paid for by our insurance!* I am the same person whether in an old Buick LeSabre or in a $52,000 brand-spanking-new Ford Expedition. The problem is that our world-colored glasses don't allow us to see it that way.

Too many times those who profess to follow Jesus don't see it that way either. As a result, we might insist on keeping up appearances. Or sink into the quagmire of the lie that our possessions, talents, intelligence, success, opportunities, careers, beauty, you-name-it, or lack thereof really do determine our worth.

Having our old Buick doesn't bother me so much with the exception of when it is incredibly hot. On those days I really would prefer a car with air conditioning. For the most part, what other people think about us in our Buick, if they ever think of us, doesn't move me. I am not often trapped in the web of needing the newest, biggest, or most expensive thing. I don't want anything else. Not when it comes to possessions. All I want to do is be able to pay my bills and not live paycheck to paycheck. There are very few things I want or need.

EXPLOSIONS OF DISCONTENT

Yet when it comes to one very particular and poignant longing, I do battle becoming disgruntled with what I do have because of what I don't have. In 2010 I finally decided I wanted to go back to school to become a theology professor. Practical theology, to be specific. But not long after I made up my mind, we became pregnant with our second, Valentina. School was out of the question.

Then, right after Valentina was born in 2012, the great heist occurred at our place of employment, a hostile takeover by religious legalists—fundamentalists who were experts at drawing fine lines in the sand. They blackmailed, bullied, abused, lied, distorted and contorted, and made many miserable to force out everybody on the wrong side of those sandy lines. It was straight out of the playbook for how fundamentalists take over, or take back, colleges and universities. And it worked like a charm despite massive student and media outcry. We were some of the many casualties. Because Shawn was the main breadwinner and Valentina a baby, his job, not mine, determined our destination.

We are so very grateful he landed a job; it is incredibly difficult for a philosophy professor to find a tenure-track job. The disadvantage, however, was location. Moving to our area put me far afield from theology PhD programs. And soon after our arrival, we had another surprise. I became pregnant with our youngest, Isabella. Giving birth to her at the end of 2014 almost killed me and put her life in jeopardy; I nearly hemorrhaged to death during delivery. But thanks be to God, we are both here. Neither Shawn nor I nor her sisters can imagine life without her.

In 2015 I finally felt well enough to start teaching a few adjunct courses at our local seminary while also working as the minister of pastoral care at our church. I loved both positions but found that teaching at the seminary combined all my interests: pastoral care, theology, ministry, history, justice, faith, and culture. I had rave reviews from the students and from higher ups. What I didn't have was a PhD. And without one I have little chance of getting a full-time job at the seminary if one should become available.

After blooming where I was planted in each place we found ourselves—after, by my own volition, joyfully and purposefully accommodating to my husband's path, and after giving birth to three beloved daughters—I finally figured out where my

"deep gladness and where the world's deep hunger meets."
And yet I have nothing to show for it.

From my vantage point, from a human standpoint, it is a
bleak outlook.

I covet.

I curse life.

I have amnesia when it comes to memento mori.

I howl in pain because I've convinced myself God has made
it easy for, loves more, and prefers more those who possess
what I desire and do not have. In such fits I trip into believing
God plays favorites and that I am not numbered among them.
I become a malcontent. God judges me to be among the rich
in this world. And I am. So why on earth do I ever feel and act
as if I am disproportionately lacking?

How distorted.

The lust of the eyes, the lust of the flesh, and the pride of
life combine with greed and covetousness to kidnap our joy.
My joy. Feeding these passions turns us into ingrates, com-
plainers. Hardhearted. Cynical. Impure. We gift our misery to
those about us.

> The lust of the eyes, the
> lust of the flesh, and the
> pride of life combine with
> greed and covetousness
> to kidnap our joy.

This raging discontent due
to my unmet longing became
internalized stress. Pressure
built. After months of chronic
stress where nearly every
possible external button of
mine was pushed, combined with hello-you've-reached-
middle-age hormonal changes, frequent and small quakes
turned into a catastrophic Mount Saint Helens–like eruption. I
blew my top. I spewed lava and volcanic ash all over my family.

It was grotesque. Not only did I have to repent, but I had to take steps to make reparations and to address the root causes leading up to it. I still am.

Like Adam and Eve, I dwell in paradise but don't acknowledge it. I regarded paradise as hell because I didn't have my *one thing*. Everything else in the garden but that one tree. No matter how hard I tried, I could do nothing to bring it about. I was powerless. Funny how I didn't realize this desire became my ring, my precious, the thing that ruled me and deformed me like Tolkien's Gollum.

Idolatry.

I was in a period of what the saints call "desolation." Father Greg Boyle, a Jesuit priest and founder of Homeboy Industries, writes, "Desolation then, is . . . not just feeling bad, but also being kept from allowing our hearts to be cradled in God's." I could sense the presence of God everywhere but in this particular, out-sized space. *What is going on?* I wondered.

ACQUIRING PEACE

Father Stephen Freeman captured the source of my epic discontent, toxic anxiety, and smothering desolation in a 2018 podcast titled "To Serve God." He observes, "And though our modern economies urge us to constant choice and variety, all of that can be a poison in our life when it enters where it doesn't belong. We lose the humility and vulnerability of acceptance, of accepting what is given." I could not bring myself to accept the given because I bought into one of the lies our market-saturated, bootstrap-pulling culture propagates: we have an endless supply of options and we can reinvent ourselves at any moment, at the drop of a hat—even in God's kingdom. Father

Stephen goes on to explain, "The illusion of choice and management also has a great propensity to create anxiety and depression. We do not have a culture of acceptance even though most of our lives lie beyond our control. We have not internalized the spiritual skill of embracing and accepting and giving thanks for what comes our way."

What Father Stephen describes is related to memento mori and our desire to be superhuman. In this situation I unknowingly white-knuckled the motto "Where there is a will, there is a way." I subconsciously trotted after the illusion of being able to do and be anything if I just set my mind to it. I was attached to a specific outcome. I tried to control and manage my life and pray in order to make it happen. For years I had set my mind to it. To me it made sense that it was the best use of my talents. Yet all the effort and mind-setting in the world could not bring it about in the way I thought it should come about. My lack of forward motion was not due to lack of effort, of time, attention, talent, energy, affirmation, or prayer. I upheld my end of the deal. Why wasn't God holding up his end of the deal? What I failed to realize is that there was no deal in the first place.

All of this roiled me and triggered latent anxiety. I could not muster the wherewithal to embrace and accept and give thanks for what was coming my way in my life. What was the sticking point? Had I grown deaf to the voice of God? Father Freeman continues, "And strangely, even the suggestion of nurturing acceptance creates a kind of anxiety in the mind of some people who say, "But we must do something!" I did fear that accepting and embracing what was given, accepting and embracing the boundaries of my life, meant I couldn't fulfill what I thought to be my calling. Why would God allow for this nonstop longing, a calling affirmed internally and externally, and fail to provide a pathway to get there? I couldn't bear it. Again, desolation. God felt a million miles away in this part of my life though not anywhere else. God was my constant companion, it seemed, until it mattered most, when the stakes were the highest.

I was, as the apostle Paul said in Acts 26:14, kicking at the goads. I was resisting God's prodding as revealed through the givenness of things: my life and circumstances. After my volcanic explosion, God and I had a come-to-Jesus moment. In exasperation I stated my case: "But look, so-and-so, and so-and-so, and so-and-so got their theology PhDs and landed in satisfying teaching posts! Why can't I?" He came back at me with "I could have easily arranged the circumstances for you to live in a city that had theology PhD programs available." I granted the omnipotent God his point. Surely such a thing was not beyond the reach of the all-powerful Creator and Sustainer of the universe.

As in other moments of my life, in this situation I had an eye only for what was lacking. I could barely detect the good. When I function in this way, I am practicing hell. Hell is laser focusing on what we don't have, refusing to take our eyes off of our deprivations. We spin them "right 'round, baby, right 'round / like a record, baby, right 'round, 'round, 'round." We ruminate. Time and eternity are swallowed up into the black hole of obsession over what we don't have.

Torment.

For me the long and the short of it is that the path I attempted, a theology PhD, doesn't appear to be the path I am to take. I don't live in a region with a university that has a theology PhD program, and I can't afford to pay out of pocket for schools in Europe. Not now at least. Why? I don't know. Misery set up residence in my life when I wedded myself to the idea that a very particular pathway was necessary to embrace my calling. When I finally, as Father Stephen Freemen pointed out, accepted the given, that God would work within the boundaries of my life, when I relinquished it all and started naming everything I did have, peace began to reign. The saints call this "consolation." Consolation is comfort from God, or as Father Boyle explains its meaning via Saint Ignatius, consolation is "any movement that propels us in the forward direction." Isn't it interesting that surrender to God moves us forward and provides consolation?

I realized I am indeed going in the direction that God wants for me at this time even if it's not the direction I thought I should be going. This is the way he has chosen.

I am learning that no matter how hard I try in any area of life, I can't channel God's grace in the direction I want it to go. God's grace carries me where God wills when God wills. Not where I will when I will. I can choose to go the direction of the river of grace or I can fight it and induce misery in myself and others. Misery in the world. For who can count how many tragedies have occurred from indulging in our ingratitude and misery?

Giving up having it our way and giving up an eye solely accustomed to focusing on what's wrong and what we don't have evaporates our ingratitude and lack of contentment. It is another way of emptying our self-will, making room for peace and contentment. It is bowing low in humility before God by offering him our hopes and dreams and our way as we wait for resurrection. *Kenōsis.*

Yes, it will demand a Herculean effort to pry our eyes and our fingers off of our agenda when it has become an idol. To once again turn to Jesus. Only then can we be filled with the grace and love of God. With Holy Spirit-assisted effort, under the direction of a spiritual director, and within community, we *can* put ourselves in a position for God to exorcise our demons and stubborn God-less self-will so that we might be filled to overflowing with gratitude, contentment, and love—even in trying circumstances. Here, I am not speaking of those who find themselves in abusive situations. If that is your circumstance, please flee to help.

From a squalid dungeon of a prison cell, probably full of roaches and rats and lice, where sleep, if it comes, doesn't come easily, Paul writes that he has learned to be content (Philippians 4:12). This, despite knowing hunger and persecution and also what it is like to have plenty. And yet he bluntly declares that being godly—being like God in our character—with contentment is great gain (1 Timothy 6:6). Interestingly enough, we can have a quite salutatory character, many vestiges of godliness, and yet be discontent.

Diana Butler Bass highlights the origins of such gratitude and contentment, "Gratitude directly emerges from a grounded life. And theologically, it emerges from an abiding trust and sense in God's presence, gifts, and abundance." Paul experienced groundedness in knowing Christ—including Christ crucified and his sufferings in each situation he was in. Paul learned to be content because he was confident in God's character. Confident in God's trustworthiness. Confident that knowing Christ was the highest good. How might I acquire godliness and contentment—peace when my good desires remain unmet?

When we've made our requests to God and done our part and accept the given until God shows us otherwise, if he ever does, we become grounded. We fix our eyes on Jesus and practice gratitude so we can learn gratitude. We live simply, as the saying goes, so others can simply live. We pray. We give thanks and cast our anxieties on the Lord. We do the next thing given to us in life. We learn a healthy detachment. We learn to listen for God's quiet voice and spot God's hands in the midst of the dizzying noise and glittering neon lights of our consumer culture. We rejoice. We think on the good, the true, and the beautiful (Philippians 4:8). We learn to be where we are, do what is given to us, expect only manna for today or for this moment.

We minimize distractions so we can hear God and give of our lives and our resources. We look to the interests of others—our local and global neighbors—and not our selfish ambitions. When you and I do this, individually and in community, the tenderness of Jesus that flooded Julian of Norwich's soul will flood our souls too so we can join her in complete assurance, believing Christ's words to her and to us: "all shall be well, and all shall be well, and all manner of thing shall be well."

It's all about getting back to the basics. These are the rhythms of *Eucharistia*, the great thanksgiving. Thanksgiving, a heart of gratitude, is the essence of communion with God and each other. Fr. Boyle reflects, "The Peruvian priest Gustavo Gutiérrez believed that only one kind of person transforms the world: the one with a grateful heart."

Indeed, our gratitude does change the world: it allows us to see and live aright. It breeds contentment. We start wherever we

> **Our gratitude does change the world: it allows us to see and live aright. It breeds contentment.**

are and practice these rhythms a little every day without comparing ourselves to others. When we lose sight of the basics and believe that we are somehow uniquely above rehearsing the fundamentals of the faith and can sidestep them without suffering the consequences, we grow discontent and bitter. Ungrounded. Professional basketball players still practice dribbling. Professional baseball players still work on their swings.

SPRING-WATCHING CHAIRS AND BOATS

I sit perched, looking out the window. My eyes happen upon what my almost seven-year-old Valentina dubbed the "Spring-Watching Chair." It is tallish for a stump, the remains of a tree, part and parcel of our new front yard. It resembles a high-backed, sitting chair at a child-sized table big enough for preschool and early elementary bottoms.

Our home sits on a corner lot and our "Spring-Watching Chair" faces outward at the corner of Cherry and South Boundary. Valentina and I thought it the perfect chair for her and for my youngest Isabella to sit and notice all the newborn blossoms and flowers and squirrels as well as other goings-on in our yard and in the yards adjacent to us.

The overstuffed chair that we acquired at garage-sale prices and in which I currently sit peering out of our window will be my "Spring-Watching Chair" even if I am inside. I can see shoots shooting up from the ground, tulips making their appearance, and white blossoms now adorning the heads of our slender trees. Fire-red berries strut about on the stage of strange bushes. I will make it my mission to inquire about the names of these bushes, strangers to me but elegant dames and damsels lining the periphery of our new home. I want to offer a curtsy, bow in gratitude for their presence and for their glorious witness to the reality of God.

Our flowers remind me of Saint John of Damascus's beautiful and astute observation, "The whole earth is a living icon of the face of God." Creation induces gratitude and wonder inside of me—contentment and groundedness too.

I watch the verdant spring arrive in splendor. I decide I am going to sit in my "Spring-Watching Chair." I'm going to hold vigil, keep an eye on what is shooting through the ground of my life. I am going to pay attention, with an eye for what I have. Furthermore, I'll keep a watchful eye on what God is doing that's new—new growth and surprises. I'll choose to choose joy. I'll open myself to surprises of joy.

It's time to restart my journal and the writing down of prayer requests and answers to prayer. In my winter of discontent, this vital rhythm of my life lay dormant. It went into a coma. It is time for stillness, time to cease striving, time to fast from eating the bread of anxiety. Time to notice again. And maybe I'll notice God noticing me.

My mind turns to Jesus sound asleep in the fishing boat while the disciples, frightened, form a bucket brigade to furiously scoop the Sea of Galilee out of their fishing boat. Any moment it would capsize, sink, hurling them into the watery mysteries of the deep. To their death. Maybe before they shake Jesus awake, they pray for a whale of a fish to come swallow them up and regurgitate them onto the shore, to save them just like one did Jonah.

Jesus in the boat is God in the flesh exhausted and sleeping but in complete control. How is it that Jesus sleeps through such chaos? Old Testament professor Scott Redd writes: "When Jesus sleeps in the hull of the boat, he does so in confidence. He doesn't lose sleep on account of weather patterns." I desire to come to the point where I generally don't "lose sleep on account of weather patterns" in this area of my life.

I use the word *generally* because perfection is not possible in this life, though I do heartily believe we can come to a point where our lives are mostly characterized by a perfect peace because our mind is stayed on God and all that flows out from him (see Isaiah 26:3). The lives of known and not as well-known saints are outstanding testimonies to this truth. It all comes down, yet again, to trust. In the context of such a struggle, Alia Joy writes, "I didn't realize I could curl up next to Jesus in the stern and find rest." I want to crawl up and curl up beside Jesus and rest with him while this storm passes instead of anxiously scooping seawater from the boat. It'll do me good. I'll become content. As the Russian Orthodox saint Seraphim of Sarov says, "Acquire the Spirit of Peace and a thousand souls around you will be saved." May it be so.

10

Incarnating the Sacred Heart of Jesus

YOUR KINGDOM COME

Do nothing out of selfish ambition or vain conceit.
Rather, in humility value others above yourselves,
not looking to your own interests but each
of you to the interests of the others.

PHILIPPIANS 2:3-4

At seventy-two, Baldemar Velasquez will tell you he learned math as a child, as a farm worker in the fields. Their Mexican-migrant farmworker family left the Rio Grande Valley of Texas wending their way up and down the East Coast, South, and Midwest on the back of a truck. They sheltered in abandoned houses or in chicken coops.

All day they suffered the most backbreaking work, stooping to harvest the food we so casually put on our tables and empty into our trash. They provided our food but barely made enough money to put food on their own table. Sometimes they went hungry. Working in the fields was a whole family affair. The children had to work if the family had any chance of eating. He remembers his mother telling him in Spanish at five or six years old, "Put a pebble in your pocket every time you fill a basket. Then you will know how many baskets you filled during the day." They were paid piece rate—paid for each basket they filled.

By the time young Baldemar was in junior high school he knew how to figure out the area of an acre, how many square feet in an acre. Math was the favorite subject of this razor-sharp mind who was awarded the MacArthur Genius Grant in 1989. One day, after they finished hoeing a field, he asked his dad, "How many acres did we hoe?" His dad said something like "thirty-five acres." Baldemar told his dad it didn't look like a thirty-five-acre field but more like a forty-acre field. He took a ruler and measured the width and the length of the field. A farmer had told his father so many rows equal an acre. What he was told was a lie. It was actually more than an acre. So, for example, they hoed forty acres but were only getting paid for thirty-five. Young Baldemar discovered they weren't getting paid for the real work they were doing. Farmers were ripping them off. However, if they protested, they would get ostracized and not get jobs with any other farmers because all the farmers in the area were friends and talked. It was a grave injustice.

Countless injustices and atrocities were committed against his fellow migrant and seasonal farmworkers despite the fact they *were* (and are) the agricultural industry in the United States. Despite their backbreaking work and primary contributions to nearly every household in the United States, he remembers reading signs posted to the door of businesses:

"No Dogs, No Negroes, No Mexicans." Finally he had the last straw when as a college student he witnessed how badly his mother and aunts and others were treated by white folk— verbally assaulted and more—and the fact that though Mexicans were the majority in the Rio Grande Valley, no Mexicans held positions of power; there were no Mexican judges, for example. Originally, he was in school to become an engineer. But he decided to transfer to Bluffton College, a Mennonite school in Northwest Ohio. There he majored in sociology. And at twenty years old he founded the Farm Labor Organizing Committee (FLOC) to defend the human rights, and especially the labor rights, of his fellow migrants.

He has worked hard all these years, for others. Even at seventy-two he has no pension. When he was asked why, he said, "How can I have a pension when none of our hard-working migrant farmworker members can barely scrape by?" He is driven by the love of Christ to serve his neighbors and also his enemies—the enemies who currently oppress him as well as the migrant farmworkers, their families, and other immigrants that we Americans continue to treat as if they were less than dogs. In fact, many treat their own dogs better.

I know this because I witness his selfless life up close. He is my boss at the Farm Labor Organizing Committee. I am intrigued by his strength, his negotiation skills, and how stalwart he is. His generosity. He will not back down. He prays about his actions. He prays for his enemies. And because of his persistence he has been a David, peacefully taking down Goliath corporations. Or rather, he has forced them to pony up justice when they would rather profiteer off of some of the literal backs of some of the poorest people in our country and the world.

Though some very famous people have sought his audience, though he has been at the table with tycoons and presidents, he doesn't treat them any differently or better than a migrant worker or community member who comes into our office asking for an appointment with him. He treats us and them with dignity, looking out for our interests too as if we are all glorious.

Through Presidente Velasquez, in our labor union made up mostly of poor migrant farm workers throughout the South and Midwest and the poor in the Toledo, Ohio, area, I am seeing the kingdom come. I am experiencing the reign and rule of Christ expanding. I am seeing Jesus walking among us, serving us from the least to the greatest.

MANY OF THE FIRST WILL BE
LAST AND THE LAST FIRST

Pastor Joanie once told Shawn and me the reason she became a United Methodist. It was because of her sister, Lynn. Lynn (who I wrote about earlier) is intellectually disabled. Decades ago, Pastor Joanie searched and searched but could not find a church who accepted Lynn for who she was, who would integrate Lynn into the life of the church. The United Methodists embraced Lynn, and so it was to the United Methodists Pastor Joanie gave her heart.

When Pastor Joanie was hired at our church, she wanted a place where Lynn and friends like her felt welcomed, where their gifts were appreciated. Our church was receptive—and a huge, vibrant ministry has grown out of Pastor Joanie's dream. The years of effort she has poured forth, along with others, in the power of the Holy Spirit has borne fruit. Intellectually disabled friends and those with other disabilities have a central place, not a marginal place, in our church. They chose a name for themselves: "Awesome God." We have an "Awesome God" Sunday school class where those of all sorts of different abilities come together as followers of Jesus. And you will find members of Awesome God as Scripture readers, ushers, greeters, or vacation Bible school helpers. We all serve alongside one another.

Shawn has often said, and I can't help but agree, that one of the main reasons our church is so warm and beautiful, so Christlike, is due to the presence, the service, and the love of the Awesome God group. They love and serve us. We love and serve them. I think of them and I think of the faces of Robbie, Kadissa, Norm, Bruce, Courtney, Tammy, and so many more.

And Pastor Joanie, the face of Christ, embodying the hospitality of God. Welcoming Shawn and me and the girls and all who come. She loves us all, each of us feels as if we are the most precious one of all to her. And we are. In Pastor Joanie we encounter the love and spaciousness of God. One of the primary ways she offers her life, in addition to offering us pastoral care and counsel, is by making room for us, by allowing us to see the love of God in her eyes. She reflects back to us just who we are in the kingdom. What an inclusive heart, bringing people into God's embrace, countering all sorts of exclusion! Her life and members of the Awesome God group are an incarnational witness reminding me that many of the last shall be first. I best pay attention.

They, the witness of their lives, serve us by continually upending our notions, judgments, prejudices, and misplaced priorities. They inspire us to live the examined life. Live and love God in the present moment. They are God's tongues of fire burning up the dross and any creeping death in our lives if we allow for it. We draw near to them and we find the kingdom among us.

THE POWER AND SERVICE OF A HOLY PRESENCE

If we turn to the book of James, which the brother of Jesus wrote, we read,

> The prayer of a righteous person is powerful and effective.
> Elijah was a human being, even as we are. He prayed earnestly that it would not rain, and it did not rain on the land for three and a half years. Again he prayed, and the heavens gave rain, and the earth produced its crops. (James 5:16-18)

James connects a holy life, a righteous life, with powerful and effective prayer. We can't miss or dismiss the connection between holiness and a powerful presence (and effective prayer!). It simply follows that the presence of holy ones is powerful and of great service to the world. I am not talking about people who claim to be holy but people who are so much like Jesus that they take our breath away. They are always looking out for the interests of others. Their selfless lives exhibit holiness without even trying because the heart and the life of Christ have been woven into the fabric of who they are. No wonder so many went out into the desert to seek out the church mothers and fathers!

Acts 19:11-12 tells us, "God did extraordinary miracles through Paul, so that even handkerchiefs and aprons that had touched him were taken to the sick, and their illnesses were cured and the evil spirits left them." Talk about a powerful presence. Of course, that power came from our Lord Jesus Christ who richly dwelled inside of Paul, an apostle, one of Jesus' disciples like you and me. Apparently, people thought the presence and power of Christ were so strong in Peter that they, "brought the sick into the streets and laid them on beds and mats so that at least Peter's shadow might fall on some of them as he passed by" (Acts 5:15).

The disciples' powerful presence and consequent service mirrored our Lord's. Remember how the woman who had been bleeding for twelve years touched the hem of Jesus' garment and was immediately healed? Remember Jesus' response? "Someone touched me; I know that power has gone out from me" (Luke 8:46). Here again we see how powerful the presence of Jesus is. All the woman did was stretch out her hand to touch the hem of his garment and she was instantly healed.

How intoxicating a thought: our very presence, our being—service. This is a fruit of living a Philippians 2 life of *kenōsis*, of making room for the mind and life of Jesus to fill us. This the fruit of Jesus' heart becoming our heart. It is a life full of the Holy Spirit. Our mere presence can usher in shalom and healing. The power of our presence can disrupt evil, initiate and build up the good. If our presence is dripping with Christ, it will drip with alluring power and also cause demons to flee.

> If our presence is dripping with Christ, it will drip with alluring power and also cause demons to flee.

This is why, mind you, the Eastern Orthodox and the Roman Catholics talk about the power of saints' relics. Saints' lives are so powerful that their bones, even after they've been long dead, are full of God's glory and radiating his power—such glory and power that miracles, healings, and a sweet-smelling fragrance are attributed to their relics. Because Christ is so deeply embedded in their bones.

I don't pretend to understand it all, and yet I can't dismiss it either. I need to repent of automatically dismissing what I know little of. I fear that studying the abuses that occurred during the Reformation under the tutelage of anti-Catholics temporarily stunted my belief, not in the miraculous but in the type of miraculous I am less familiar with. It led to unseeing, blindness.

But now I pay attention to what my holy sisters and brothers have to say even if I haven't experienced it myself. We all know that our lack of experience cannot render another's testimony false. At least we *should* know that. Brothers and sisters in other countries would have no qualms about testifying to such miracles and also to demonic opposition. Do we forget that we "wrestle not against flesh and blood" (see Ephesians 6:12 KJV) and that God is "able to do immeasurably more than all we ask or imagine, according to his power that is at work within us" (Ephesians 3:20)?

Like Roman Catholics, for millennia the Eastern Orthodox have held fast to the miraculous power of the presence of a soul deeply steeped in the love and power of Christ. I have to confess that more and more I think many of us, in richer countries at least, have a stunted divine imagination and thus a stunted experience of the power of God. "And he did not many mighty works there because of their unbelief" (Matthew 13:58 KJV).

REMINDERS OF WHAT MATTERS MOST

A life emptied of our own agenda in favor of God's is a powerful presence, a servant life, never limited by our education, privileges, worldly possessions, or lack thereof. We sat in church on

Pentecost and Pastor Russ reminded us that throughout the Gospels we see the disciples jockeying for position. They argued about who would be the greatest in the coming kingdom. But Jesus turns it around on them and on us. Translating Jesus' words to us, Pastor Russ called our attention to the teaching of the Lord: "The disciples—and we—think it's about getting the best seat at the table, the place of honor, the position of power and prestige and popularity. But Jesus left the table, lowered himself, stooped down, and washed their feet."

Jesus did the work of a servant because no one else wanted to do it. God himself showed us that he is not too great to humble himself. Behold divine humiliation, the love of God! What king would bow to wash the stinky, filthy feet of poor subjects? Our God! Once more I think of Charles de Foucauld's words: "Jesus has so diligently searched for the lowest place that it would be very difficult for anyone to tear it from him."

> A life emptied of our own agenda in favor of God's is a powerful presence.

And so his words to his disciples and to us once more are: "Now that I, your Lord and Teacher, have washed your feet, you also should wash one another's feet. I have set you an example that you should do as I have done for you" (John 13:14-15). Jesus demonstrated in word and deed that "Anyone who wants to be first must be the very last, and the servant of all" (Mark 9:35).

Pastor Russ finished with a personal story about a memorable encounter he had with a homeless man. At the time he was not a pastor; rather, he worked as a regional manager for a drugstore in the Cincinnati area. One day, as he was waiting for the signal at a crosswalk on a busy downtown street, a homeless man approached him and asked for something to eat. Russ quickly spotted a hotdog cart across the street. Together, they walked over to the cart. Russ bought a couple of hotdogs and Cokes, and they ate lunch together there on the street. As they talked, the homeless man, quite out of nowhere, asked Russ about his life in Christ. Out of this homeless man's mouth, whose name God is well aware of even though we aren't, spilled the good news of the gospel. Look at how it works: Pastor Russ shared physical sustenance or food, and the homeless man shared his food, his spiritual sustenance—God's Word and life.

Don't miss it: Russ served him by sharing a meal and lunchtime conversation. And he—though being homeless, or maybe because of it—became a powerful spiritual presence who served Russ. And this man, though he knows it not, has served us because we are some of the beneficiaries of this story. Pentecost.

We always need the reminder. The people we ignore because they don't seem worth our time and attention? Because they aren't famous enough or at all, aren't rising stars or at the top of whatever game we wish to play? They may be a beggar at the gate of an estate, a janitor, maid, taxi driver, immigrant, elder living alone or in a nursing home, prisoner, or a child. These precious ones could very well be kings or queens in the kingdom come.

THE FRUIT: THE KINGDOM, SALVATION, GLORY OF GOD EVERLASTING

If we catch this vision, if God is our vison, if you and I follow hard after Christ, if we renounce the world and the devil and remember our baptisms, if we love God and love our neighbors by serving them—if our presence is present in the form of a kenotic life, a self-giving life—then dynamite Pentecost power will come. It will come whether or not we are conscious of it, and at times it will come in disguise. Look for it among the humble and the good. Look for it among the Christlike. If we *survey the wondrous cross on which our Prince of glory died, and count our richest gains, loss, and pour contempt on all our pride*. If we put ourselves in a posture to receive his kingdom, it will come in and through us and also despite us.

In living a kenotic life, we will see glimpses of the kingdom now in the land of the living, and testify with Jesus' mother Mary and all the saints once the kingdom comes in all its fullness, that

> In living a kenotic life, we will see glimpses of the kingdom now in the land of the living.

> My soul glorifies the Lord
> 　and my spirit rejoices in God my Savior,
> for he has been mindful
> 　of the humble state of his servant.
> From now on all generations will call me blessed,
> 　for the Mighty One has done great things for me—
> 　holy is his name.
> His mercy extends to those who fear him,
> 　from generation to generation.
> He has performed mighty deeds with his arm;
> 　he has scattered those who are proud in their inmost
> 　　thoughts.
> He has brought down rulers from their thrones
> 　but has lifted up the humble.

He has filled the hungry with good things
   but has sent the rich away empty.
He has helped his servant Israel,
   remembering to be merciful
to Abraham and his descendants forever,
   just as he promised our ancestors. (Luke 1:46-55)

What power of Christ is present in a holy life! What great offerings to God, and the world on his behalf, will occur the more the heart of Jesus is formed in us! There is no telling! And we probably will never know. That is best, I think, lest we be tempted to lay claim to God's glory. God calls us to stoop. Like Jesus, like the farmworkers who stoop to put our food on the table, we are to stoop, to serve that our lives might be Eucharist for the world. Like Thérèse of Lisieux, let our joy be found in our service being the sweet-smelling flowers we strew along God's path! As we stoop, as we serve, as we strew flowers in God's path, God wills and works in and through his powerful presence in us and throughout the whole church to do his good pleasure (Philippians 2:13). This is part of the way his kingdom comes, by our living a life of self-offering, *kenōsis*, of being the servant of all—just like Jesus. Let us together stoop and serve. As the *Didache*, some of the earliest teaching in the church, says,

Let grace come and let this world pass away. Hosannah to the God of David. If any man be holy, let him come! If any man be not, let him repent: Maranatha ("Our Lord! Come!"), Amen.

Acknowledgments

I could not have done this without my best friend in the world and constant companion and wise counselor and favorite person on the earth for millions of reasons: my husband, Shawn. These aforementioned words are pretty paltry to describe the depth of gratitude, love, and admiration I have for him as well as the help he has given. This book would not be here without him. My life and love and joy go out to my three beautiful, brilliant, creative, and dearly beloved daughters, gifts of God: Iliana, Valentina, and Isabella. I choose you every time. Thank you for your patience with Mommy as I have spent many a day and night writing and revising. I love you.

I want to thank my mom and dad, Myrna and J. R. Proper, for all the love and patience they have shown me—for what I didn't understand as a child and for showing me it's possible to experience lots of suffering and still be generous and others-oriented. My deepest love and admiration for my siblings who are also in the best friend category—Michelle, Kenny, and Marco—who love me because of me and despite me. I am so grateful to my mother-in-law, Trudy Graves, for watching our girls and supporting us in innumerable ways—for loving us in word and deed. Also to my brother-in-law, Chris, sister-in-law, Michelle, and nephew, Brendan—you bring great joy and laughter and fun into our lives.

Many thanks, InterVarsity Press, for believing me since way back when. You have sought me out for years and rooted for me even when I was with another publisher. Thank you, Jeff Crosby and my editor, Cindy Bunch, for your magnanimous encouragement and for all of you who work so hard at IVP to bring this and other good books out into the world. We notice.

Michelle Van Loon, Alison Hodgson, Debby Smith: you read the first few chapter drafts of this manuscript and then encouraged me to keep on with this book. You launched me. I also want to thank Catherine Carlson McNeil, my brother Kenny and his wife Chelsea, and others who faithfully prayed for me and my writing. I've had two spiritual directors help guide me through too: Sister Diane and Suzanne—many and eternal thanks.

The individuals in these groups and churches have carried me: The OKJFC, Her.meneutics, INK: A Creative Collective, Redbud Writers Guild, Chapmanville Community Church, Rochester Christian Reformed Church, Midtown (church plant), Olentangy CRC, FBC Dayton, St. Andrews UMC in Findlay, Maumee UMC, our Wednesday night prayer group, the writers and editors at Our Daily Bread Ministries, the Farm Labor Organizing Committee (FLOC), Northeastern Seminary, the students and staff at Winebrenner Seminary, Ancient Faith Radio, Lisa Sharon Harper and the Ruby Woo Pilgrimage pilgrims, Latina writers on Facebook and Twitter, and Renovaré.

I have deep gratitude for Pastor Larry Kreps and his wife, Marti, Emily Boerger and Ben Dolan, Randi Stolick, Aaron and

Danielle Van Fleet, Karla and John Dennis, Heidi Corbin, Debra Arce, Donna Beasely, Dana Leader, Deb Guthrie, John and Jennifer Burns, Nancy Weakly, Rod and Johnelle Kennedy, Jason Alspaugh, Jen Castellani, and David Olsen for being our friends and supporting us while we were in and emerging from the wilderness and beyond. You were good Samaritans to my family and me when we were left for dead. I will always remember. We came to life, and I emerged to write this.

Our dear friends that we 9-1-1 for support and who have gone the distance with us in the last five years:

Carl and Debby Smith
Carmille Akande
Christina and Brandon Lute
Kim and Chad Deakyne
Bob and Jan Arbogast
Jeff and Inge Cook
Susan Green
Helen Bass
Mario and Tera Alejandre
Amy Saylor
Christy and Ryan Peterson
Michelle Van Loon
Russ and Michelle Tichenor
Joanie Schilling
Mama Carol Hinde
Margaret and Bill Wheeler
Dave and Rebecca Mills
Christine Fulmer
Juli Furj-Kuhn
Michael and Larissa Pahl

Aaron and Jessica James
Julie Moore
Callie Glorioso-Mays
Jerilyn Cox Hoover
Katie and Riley Livermore
Ellen Moore
Julita Bailey-Vasco
Jessica Robb
Laura Dryer
Lyndsey Gvora Brennan
Chris and Krista Sellers
Jen Pollock Michel
Karen Swallow Prior
Rachel Marie Stone
Jennifer Grant
Caryn Dashland-Rivadeneira
Sharon Hodde Miller
Ellen Painter Dollar
Haley Gray Scott
Laura Turner

Lesa Engelthaler

Alison Hodgson

Jessica Mesman-Griffith

Dale Hanson-Bourke

Tyler John

Blake and Rebekah Hereth

Andy and Anne Zell

David Baldwin

Barb Stewart

Mary Bailey

Brian Hinde

Rachel Barkholz

Irma Ayers

Gina Dalfonzo

The members of our small group: Jenna West, Carolyn Ford, Michelle Klewer, Marlene Roloff, Gwynn and Allen Drown, Lisa Levi, Bill Stewart.

If I have inadvertently forgotten someone, know I hold you. God knows. There are so many friends on Twitter that I hope to meet in person too—you've encouraged me for so long. And all the students, love to you!

Finally, I want to extend my heartfelt thanks to you, the reader, for reading my words. It is a great honor.

Notes

1 SELF-EMPTYING: THE MYSTERY OF OUR SALVATION

2 *That is how I treat my friends*: St. Teresa of Ávila as quoted by Dorothy Day, *The Long Loneliness: The Autobiography of the Legendary Catholic Social Activist* (New York: HarperOne, 1952), 140.

I take my permission to speak freely: I love the title and concept of Anne Jackson's book *Permission to Speak Freely* (Nashville: Thomas Nelson, 2010).

3 *You are always on my mind*: The words to Willy Nelson's "Always on My Mind" are *"You were always on my mind."* Wayne Carson, Johnny Christopher, Mark James, "Always on My Mind," 1970.

4 *When God is silent and darkness covers*: God the Father did not answer God the Son on the cross when Jesus cried, "My God, my God, why have you forsaken me?" (Matthew 27:45-46).

6 *a less-distorted image of him*: I'm thankful for Father Phillip LeMaster for giving me the word *distorted* in his podcast titled "Light of the World," *Eastern Christian Insights*, July 25, 2018, www.ancientfaith.com/podcasts/easternchristian insights/the_light_of_the_world.

9 *Many people feel that they could achieve*: Caryll Houselander, *The Reed of God* (Allen, TX: Christian Classics, 1944), 18-19.

10 *If we are to be transformed*: Stephen Freeman, "The Church and the Cross of Christ," *Glory to God in All Things* (blog), accessed December 7, 2017, https://fatherstephen.word press.com/2011/05/13/the-church-and-the-cross-of-christ.

2 DOWN LOW WITH JESUS

13 *None of us knows*: The first eight paragraphs of this chapter is taken from Marlena Graves, "The Place of Privilege in the Kingdom of God," *Mudroom* (blog), June 24, 2016, http://mudroomblog.com/privilege-kingdom-of-god/.

17 *the lowest place: the place of the poor*: Carlo Carretto, *Essential Writings*, ed. Robert Ellsberg (New York: Orbis Books, 2007), 60.

18 *Charles de Foucauld*: In Carlo Carretto, *Essential Writings*, ed. Robert Ellsberg (New York: Orbis Books, 2007), 60.

25 *Growing up and even into my adulthood*: The last section of this chapter is taken from Graves, "The Place of Privilege in the Kingdom of God."

3 ALL FLAME

30 *Klansman, take a picture in a choir loft:* DeNeen L. Brown, "The Preacher Who Used Christianity to Revive the Ku Klux Klan," *Washington Post*, April 10, 2018, www.washingtonpost.com /news/retropolis/wp/2018/04/08/the-preacher-who-used -christianity-to-revive-the-ku-klux-klan/.

the town's butcher, baker, candlestick maker: Brown, "The Preacher Who Used Christianity." I am taking some creative license in imagining the careers of these men, but I am not far from the truth. You can do the research and see that law enforcement and pastors were part of the Ku Klux Klan. For example, in her *Washington Post* article Brown recounted the story of William Joseph Simmons: "It was approaching midnight on Oct. 16, 1915, when Methodist preacher William Joseph Simmons and at least 15 other men climbed Stone Mountain in Georgia. They built an altar, set fire to a cross, took an oath of allegiance to the 'Invisible Empire' and announced the revival of the Ku Klux Klan. Beneath a makeshift altar glowing in the flickering flames of the burning cross, they laid a U.S. flag, a sword and a Holy Bible. 'The angels that have anxiously watched the reformation from its beginnings,' said Simmons, who declared himself Imperial Wizard, 'must have hovered about Stone Mountain and shouted hosannas to the highest heavens.'"

32 *I love the pure, peaceable, and impartial Christianity*: Frederick Douglass, quoted in Noel Rae, "How Christian Slaveholders Used the Bible to Justify Slavery," *Time*, February 23, 2018, http://time.com/5171819/christianity-slavery -book-excerpt.

32 *1 John 2:9-11*: In the NIV this passage is a simple paragraph. I have set it off in poetic form.

34 *To understand Jesus' teachings*: Dallas Willard, *The Divine Conspiracy: Rediscovering Our Hidden Life in God* (San Francisco: Harper One, 1997), 232.

35 *We cannot... love God and hate*: Willard, *Divine Conspiracy*, 232.

39 *It is a brutal experience*: For more on this see my book *A Beautiful Disaster: Finding Hope in the Midst of Brokenness* (Grand Rapids: Brazos, 2014).

40 *the needs of the villagers in Turkana County, Kenya*: I spoke with Fr. Nick Louh on the phone on May 28, 2019, to confirm the details of this story.

43 *To be living a spiritual life, you cannot simply pray*: Evan Armatas, phone conversation I had on his radio show, *Orthodoxy Live*, on May 12, 2019.

If your prayer doesn't include fasting: Evan Armatas, phone conversation.

44 *God, there's hopeless apathy in my bones*: Laura Jean Truman (@LauraJeanTruman), "God, there's hopeless apathy in my bones," Twitter, August 6, 2019, https://twitter.com/LauraJeanTruman/status/1158937023316713472. Used with permission.

4 DAILY RETURNING HOME

48 *It's me, it's me, O Lord*: "Standing in the Need," an African American spiritual of unknown origin. It first appeared in *The Book of American Negro Spirituals* (1925), compiled by James Weldon Johnson and J. Rosamond Johnson, https://hymnary.org/text/not_my_brother_nor_my_sister_but_its_me.

49 *a cold self-righteous prig*: C. S. Lewis, *Mere Christianity* (New York: Macmillan, 1952), 95.

50 *It is easy indeed to confess that I have not fasted*: Alexander Schmemann, *Great Lent: Journey to Pascha* (Yonkers, NY: St. Vladamir's Seminary Press, 1974), 21-22, https://sttimothy-toccoa.org/files/Inquirers/Chap1.pdf.

51 *recycling my swords into plowshares*: Eugene Peterson, *The Pastor* (New York: HarperCollins, 2011), 79.

51 *I've been a whistleblower and have endured*: See chapter five of my book, *A Beautiful Disaster: Finding Hope in the Midst of Brokenness* (Grand Rapids: Brazos, 2014).

53 *a critical awareness and a sure watch over oneself*: Vassilios Papavasilliou, *Thirty Steps to Heaven: The Ladder of Divine Ascent for All Walks of Life* (Chesterton, IN: Ancient Faith Publishing, 2013), 47.

55 *steps 5-10 here*: "The Twelve Steps of Alcoholics Anonymous," Acoholics Anonymous, accessed December 31, 2018, www.alcoholics-anonymous.org.uk/about-aa/the-12-steps-of-aa.

57 *Tradition holds that Al-Maghtas*: "Baptism Site 'Bethany Beyond the Jordan' (Al-Maghtas)," UNESCO, accessed January 1, 2019, https://whc.unesco.org/en/list/1446.

60 *It is true, that open enmity, personal hatred*: Alexander Schmemann, "Forgiveness Sunday," Orthodox Church in America, March 1, 2014, https://oca.org/reflections/fr-alexander-schmemann/forgiveness-sunday.

5 DO YOU SEE WHAT I SEE?: TRANSFIGURATION

66 *Sarah Smith of Golders Green*: C. S. Lewis, *The Great Divorce*, rev. ed. (San Francisco: HarperOne, 1973), 117-19.

70 *freely making his will subservient*: "Very truly I tell you," Jesus tells us, "the Son can do nothing by himself; he can do only what he sees his Father doing, because whatever the Father does the Son also does" (John 5:19).

75 *You mean, God looks* happy *at me?*: A version of this story can be found in my devotional "Happy at You," *Our Daily Journey*, October 26, 2016, www.ourdailyjournal.beta.ourdailybread.org/2016/10/26/happy-at-you.

6 OUR TEACHERS: MESSENGERS OF GRACE

79 *Why are folks homeless in the first place*: John H. Flores, "What Kind of Society Do We Want to Live In?" Social Justice Institute, July 17, 2017, www.youtube.com/watch?v=-hsV4sTjcr4.

83 *The rich man doesn't want to contact Lazarus*: Stanley Hauerwas and Jean Vanier, *Living Gently in a Violent World: The Prophetic Witness of Weakness* (Downers Grove, IL: InterVarsity Press, 2008), 66.

87 *we look down on others*: See Sally Lloyd-Jones, *Jesus Story-book Bible* (Grand Rapids: Zondervan, 2007), 285.

89 *I will be far away from the VIP seats*: Someone implanted this picture of us being near or far during that great feast. I want to say it could've been the late Ed Dobson of Calvary Church in Grand Rapids, Michigan, when he visited my college in 1996. If it was someone else I heard, my apologies. I am open to correction and to making the attribution to that person.

7 RICH TOWARD GOD

93 *low social class participants were more generous*: Utpal Dholakia, "Why People Who Have Less Give More," *Psychology Today*, November 20, 2017, www.psychologytoday.com/us/blog/the-science-behind-behavior/201711/why-people-who-have-less-give-more.

94 *we give it all up to "possess God"*: Clement of Alexandria, "Who Is the Rich Man That Shall Be Saved?" *New Advent*, accessed November 1, 2019, www.newadvent.org/fathers/0207.htm.

95 *The bread in your cupboard*: Basil the Great, "On Almsgiving," St. George Orthodox Church Ministries, accessed December 11, 2019, https://www.stgeorgepantry.org/almsgiving1.

Members of the early church were especially renown: Gary B. Ferngren, "A New Era in Roman Healthcare," *Christian History* 101 (2011), https://christianhistoryinstitute.org/magazine/article/new-era-in-roman-healthcare.

96 *Cyprian of Carthage "enjoined the city's Christians to give aid"*: Ferngren, "A New Era in Roman Healthcare."

97 *to live in "unapologetic opulence"*: Neil Genzlinger, "Robin Leach, 76, 'Lifestyles of the Rich and Famous' Host, Dies," *New York Times*, August 24, 2018, www.nytimes.com/2018/08/24/obituaries/robin-leach-dead-lifestyles-rich-famous.html.

Pope Francis who choose to live in a simple residence: Mauro Bazzucchi, "While Pope Francis Lives in a Dorm, U.S. Bishops Enjoy Italian Luxury," *HuffPost*, updated March 5,

2016, www.huffpost.com/entry/us-bishops-italy-residence-luxuryf_n_56cf696de4b0bf0dab315eba.

98 *Store them in our closet until that person in need is in front of us*: Marie Kondo, who advocates simple and clutter-free living and tossing out anything that doesn't spark joy, won't mind. See "Mari Kondo," *Wikipedia*, accessed November 1, 2019, https://en.wikipedia.org/wiki/Marie_Kondo.

Let thine alms sweat into thine hands: Didache 1.6, *Didache*, accessed June 8, 2019, www.thedidache.com. The *Didache* was an early catechism also known as the *Teaching of the Twelve Apostles*. It dates to the first century.

100 *modesty is "freedom from vanity and conceit"*: "Modesty," *OneLook Thesaurus*, accessed June 1, 2019, www.onelook. com/thesaurus/?s=modesty.

101 *When Wesley died, he had nothing on earth*: Randy Alcorn, "John Wesley's Example of Giving," *Eternal Perspective Ministries*, May 14, 2014, www.epm.org/blog/2014/May/14/john-wesley-giving.

Wesley preached that Christians: Charles Edward White, quoted in Alcorn, "John Wesley's Example of Giving."

103 *Most of my students go hungry*: Isaac Moore, email to the author, May 29, 2019.

8 MEMENTO MORI

105 *have the expectation of death daily before one's eyes*: St. Benedict, *The Rule of St. Benedict* (London: SPCK, 1931), 6, www.solesmes.com/sites/default/files/upload/pdf/rule_of_st_benedict.pdf.

106 *at the sight of three wilted roses*: My husband, Shawn, still buys roses for each of our daughters on their birthdays (and on Valentine's Day). A rose for each year of life.

109 *Saint Francis of Assisi once signed a blessing*: Theresa Aletheia Noble, "Momento Mori: How a Skull on Your Desk Will Change Your Life," *Aleteia*, September 12, 2017, https://aleteia.org/2017/09/12/memento-mori-how-a-skull-on-your-desk-will-change-your-life.

110 *Dance of Death*: Ashby Kinch, "How the Dead Danced with the Living in Medieval Society," *Crux*, October 31, 2017,

https://cruxnow.com/global-church/2017/10/31/dead-danced-living-medieval-society.

116 *In Christian theology,* kairos *is*: McKinley Valentine, "Whereof We Cannot Speak, Thereof We Must Remain Silent," *Chronos & Kairos* (blog), accessed December 11, 2019, https://mckinleyvalentine.com/kairos.

117 *Henri Nouwen talks about it too*: One of my favorite books is Henri Nouwen's book *In the Name of Jesus* (Chestnut Ridge, NY: Crossroad, 1992).

9 CRADLED IN THE HEART OF GOD: GRATITUDE AND CONTENTMENT

127 *deep gladness and where the world's deep hunger meets*: Frederick Buechner, "Vocation," *Frederick Buechner* (blog), July 18, 2017, www.frederickbuechner.com/quote-of-the-day/2017/7/18/vocation.

128 *Desolation then, is . . . not just feeling bad*: Greg Boyle, *Barking to the Choir: The Power of Radical Kinship* (New York: Simon & Schuster, 2017), 115.

And though our modern economies urge us: Stephen Freeman, "To Serve God," *Ancient Faith Ministries*, February 3, 2018, www.ancientfaith.com/podcasts/freeman/to_serve_god.

129 *The illusion of choice and management*: Freeman, "To Serve God."

I could not muster the wherewithal: Freeman, "To Serve God."

But we must do something!: Freeman, "To Serve God."

130 *right 'round, baby, right 'round*: Pete Burns et al., "You Spin Me Round (Like A Record)," *Youthquake*, Epic, 1985.

131 *consolation is "any movement that propels us"*: Gregory Boyle, *Barking to the Choir*, 115.

132 *please flee to help*: I never ever advocate staying in abusive situations or that an abusive situation is the cross one must take up. Here I am speaking of nonabusive situations. I want to make that clear.

132   *Gratitude directly emerges from a grounded life*: Diana Butler Bass, "A Lecture on Gratitude," *Living the Questions*, March 1, 2018, https://vimeo.com/262263324.

133   *all shall be well, and all shall be well*: Julian of Norwich, *Revelations of Divine Love*, trans. Diane Warrack (1901), chap. 27, www.ccel.org/ccel/julian/revelations.xiv.i.html.

     The Peruvian priest Gustavo Gutiérrez: Boyle, *Barking to the Choir*, 119.

135   *The whole earth is a living icon*: John of Damascus, quoted in Benedict XVI, "The Whole Earth Is a Living Icon of the Face of God," Oblates of St. Benedict, December 4, 2014, http://oblatesosbbelmont.org/2014/12/04/the-whole-earth -is-a-living-icon-of-the-face-of-god.

136   *Jesus sleeps in the hull of the boat*: Scott Redd, "Why Did Jesus Sleep During the Storm?" *Gospel Coalition*, January 8, 2019, www.thegospelcoalition.org/article/jesus-sleep-storm.

     I didn't realize I could curl up next to Jesus: Alia Joy, quoted in Kate Motaung, "FMF Writing Prompt Link-up: Lack," *Five Minute Friday*, April 11, 2019, https://fiveminutefriday.com /2019/04/11/fmf-writing-prompt-link-up-lack.

     Acquire the Spirit of Peace and a thousand souls: Seraphim of Sarov, quoted in Stephen Freeman, "What St. Seraphim Meant," *Glory to God for All Things* (blog), September 17, 2007, https://blogs.ancientfaith.com/glory2godforallthings /2007/09/17/what-st-seraphim-meant.

10 INCARNATING THE SACRED HEART OF JESUS: YOUR KINGDOM COME

145   *Jesus has so diligently searched*: Carlo Carretto, *Essential Writings*, ed. Robert Ellsberg (New York: Orbis Books, 2007), 60.

147   *If we survey the wondrous cross*: These word are taken from Isaac Watts, "When I Survey the Wondrous Cross," 1707.

148   *Let grace come and let this world pass away*: Didache 10.6, *Didache*, accessed June 8, 2019, www.thedidache.com.